Holiday Fare

Holiday Fare

FAVORITE WILLIAMSBURG RECIPES

By John R. Gonzales

Tom Green, photographer

Colonial Williamsburg

The Colonial Williamsburg Foundation
Williamsburg, Virginia

© 2004 by The Colonial Williamsburg Foundation

Published 2004

Printed in Singapore

15 14 13 12 11 10 09 08 07 06 05   2 3 4 5 6 7 8 9 10

Library of Congress Cataloging-in-Publication Data

Gonzales, John R.
    Holiday fare : favorite Williamsburg recipes / by John R. Gonzales ;
Tom Green, photographer.— 1st ed.
      p. cm.
    Includes index.
    ISBN 978-0-87935-196-0 (hardcover : alk. paper)
    1. Holiday cookery. 2. Cookery—Virginia—Williamsburg. I. Title.
    TX739.G596 2004
    641.5'68'097554252—dc22
                            2004011884

Book and jacket design by Helen M. Olds

Food styling by Cathy B. Hinton

Food photography art direction by Helen M. Olds

Additional photography by David M. Doody and staff of
The Colonial Williamsburg Foundation

Properties by Susan Hight Rountree

Frontispiece: Gala fireworks usher in the holiday season.

*Colonial Williamsburg is a registered trade name of
The Colonial Williamsburg Foundation, a not-for-profit
educational institution.*

The Colonial Williamsburg Foundation
PO Box 1776
Williamsburg, VA 23187-1776
www.colonialwilliamsburg.org

for Nancy

Contents

My earliest memory of cooking was baking Christmas cookies with my grandma Emily in the basement kitchen of The Blue Bell tavern in Colonial Williamsburg's Historic Area. The Blue Bell, on the eastern green of the Capitol building, had originally been an eighteenth-century "ordinary," a kind of tavern that specialized in the practice of serving meals. Some 250 years later, The Blue Bell was my home and my grandmother had come from Nebraska to spend the holidays. We baked sugar cookies cut into festive shapes and sprinkled them with red and green decorating sugars. My family later moved "uptown" into the Robert Carter House, next door to the Governor's Palace, where we lived for the next twenty years.

Introduction

This book celebrates a season, the bounty of the holiday table, and a special place called home with its history and foods that have inspired these recipes. There is also a personal, everlasting celebration from my good fortune of growing up in the wonderful little village known as Colonial Williamsburg's Historic Area. As a youngster I became immersed in a sanctum of early American heritage, with colonial homes and gardens, and Williamsburg's culture so alive with the tradition of southern hospitality. Here the holiday season is a glorious time that has helped define the meaning of shared American traditions for centuries.

My early years bestowed on me a rich personal history filled with childhood memories and indescribable yet vivid sensory recollections. It is impossible to separate the excitement of the holiday season from the spirit of Colonial Williamsburg's unique traditions. For me, Thanksgiving brings not only family time and meals but also the start of preparations for the holidays: the festiveness of trimming homes with fresh wreaths and ropings of white pine, the trees decorated, and all windows glowing with candlelight.

In Colonial Williamsburg's Historic Area, the holidays officially commence with Grand Illumination, a thrilling experience that has not changed much since the time it was originally called White Lighting. At the Robert Carter House, my parents always planned their own Grand Illumination party. It was the only way to have enough people on hand to simultaneously light each and every window candle when the marshall of the parade would announce, "Mr. Carter, light your candles!" At that moment, everyone would twist the bulbs tight in their sockets and be off to the streets and Market Square to partake in the festivities.

Then as now at Grand Illumination the streets and common areas, alight with burning cressets, resound with the fifes and drums and the booming of cannons and musket fire. Grand Illumination reaches a crescendo with a display of glorious fireworks. Visitors and townspeople alike enjoy holiday fare with hot buttered rums, toddies and grogs served at the taverns, and Raleigh Tavern gingerbread cookies dunked in hot apple cider served beside open bonfires.

Grand Illumination is not just a single day of celebration, but heralds the first day of a season: it ushers in Christmastide. The celebration of a colonial Christmas past continues through Christmas Day and the New Year. The calendar is filled with seasonal museum exhibitions, decoration demonstrations, and numerous Christmastide adventures for children. Concerts, plays, caroling, strolling balladeers, the diversion of dance, and yuletide strings help define the singular experience of a Colonial Williamsburg Christmas. The revelry is crowned by relishing distinctive seasonal dishes that embody the shared Southern culinary heritage.

The phenomenon of the American experience with holiday food is more than a yen for the familiar. The ingredients that Mother Nature offers up feeds a physiological reaction that leads to a craving for certain foods and flavors at particular times. Jean Anthelme Brillat-Savarin, French gastronome and contemporary of Thomas Jefferson, wrote, "Taste, such as it is by the grace of nature, remains the one among our senses, when everything is taken into consideration, which procures us the maximum of delight . . . It invites us, by way of the pleasure derived, to make good the losses which we suffer in the activities of life."

Living in a fast-paced world makes modern Americans yearn for what is dependable and secure. Every year the holiday season extends a welcome relief, offering up an oasis of comfort called tradition. In Colonial Williamsburg's Historic Area, friends, family, and visitors experience the simpler life of the eighteenth century, finding a touchstone of unchanging seasonal traditions that define southern hospitality and illuminate the spirit of the holidays, past and present.

In writing the recipes for this cookbook, I delighted in the challenge of balancing my personal temptation to be creative as a chef with my commitment to the time-honored culinary traditions of the season. The recipes in *Holiday Fare* are inspired by mostly indigenous ingredients from the harvest season that have documented historical relevance.

For me, the enjoyment of the holidays boils down to the food shared around the family table. My favorite recipe in this book is the roasted turkey, not so much for its moist meat and crispy skin, but because it translates into all the beloved side dishes and good cheer of which the turkey is the centerpiece. All year long my family thinks about the next time we will have corn pudding, oyster stuffing, and "bourboned" mashed sweet potatoes.

I agree with Fernand Point, the renowned twentieth-century French chef, when he said, "If the divine creator has taken pains to give us delicious and exquisite things to eat, the least we can do is prepare them well and serve them with ceremony."

What better time than the holidays to live by those words and celebrate.

"When it grew too dark to dance . . . we conversed til half after six; Nothing is now to be heard of in conversation, but the Balls, *the* Fox-hunts, *the fine* entertainments, *and the* good fellowship, *which are to be exhibited at the approaching* Christmas.*"*
    —Philip Vickers Fithian, tutor to the Robert Carter children, in his journal December 18, 1773

Appetizers and Hors d'Oeuvres

Now *Christmas* comes, 'tis fit that we

Should feast and sing, and merry be

Keep open House, let Fiddlers play

A Fig for Cold, sing Care away

And may they who thereat repine

On brown Bread and on small Beer dine.

—*Virginia Almanack*, 1766

In Martha Washington's record of family "receipts," TO MAKE AN HARTICHOAK PIE states: "Take 12 hartychoak bottoms that are good & large; after you have boyled them, take them cleere from the leaves & cores, season them with a little pepper & salt, & lay them in a coffin of paste, with a pound of butter." Baking artichokes into a savory pie remains a favorite in southern kitchens today. This modern adaptation retains the English influence while spicing up the crust with black pepper and paprika.

Savory Artichoke and Cheddar Cheese Pie with Pepper Crust

Serves 8

1 pie dough recipe (see page 17), or 1 (9-inch) deep-dish-style piecrust
1 teaspoon coarsely ground or cracked black pepper
1 teaspoon paprika
1 tablespoon butter
1 tablespoon extra-virgin olive oil
1 medium onion, finely chopped (about 1 cup)
2 (8-ounce) packages cream cheese, softened
2 (14-ounce) cans artichoke hearts, drained and chopped into 1/2-inch pieces
2 eggs, lightly beaten
1 cup grated cheddar cheese
1/2 cup shredded parmesan cheese
1/2 cup fresh bread crumbs (about 2 slices bread)
1/2 cup chopped green onions
1 teaspoon salt
1/8 teaspoon cayenne pepper

Prepare the pie dough, adding the black pepper and paprika into the sifted flour and salt. If using a premade piecrust, press the black pepper and paprika into the crust.

Melt the butter with the olive oil in a medium-sized heavy-duty skillet over medium-high heat.

Add the onions and cook, stirring often, 3 to 5 minutes, or until softened. Transfer the onions to a large mixing bowl.

Gently blend the cream cheese and onions with an electric mixer on low speed until smooth.

Mix the artichokes into the cream cheese mixture using a wooden spoon.

Stir in the eggs, cheddar cheese, parmesan cheese, bread crumbs, green onions, salt, and cayenne pepper until thoroughly mixed.

Preheat the oven to 425 degrees.

Roll out the dough onto a floured surface large enough to line a deep-dish-style 9-inch pie pan and decoratively crimp the edges. Refrigerate until the oven is fully preheated.

Place the artichoke mixture in the dough-lined pan or piecrust.

Bake for 15 minutes, then reduce the heat to 350 degrees. Bake about 35 to 40 additional minutes, or until it is golden brown and the center of the pie is just set.

Cool on a wire rack. Serve a large wedge with toast rounds or crackers as an hors d'oeuvre or a small wedge as an individual serving.

Southern hospitality is brought to life by serving all kinds of nut dishes during the holidays. This recipe features large, indigenous pecans candied with leeks. The caramelized flavors and crisp textures meld deliciously over creamy brie cheese. Garnishing this appetizer with red and green grapes makes it a perfect holiday centerpiece.

Candied Pecans and "Leek-y" Brie

Serves 8 to 10

1/2 cup sugar
2 tablespoons butter
3/4 cup roughly chopped jumbo pecan
   halves (about 4 ounces)
1/8 teaspoon salt
1 small leek, most of green discarded,
   sliced, and rinsed (about 1 cup)
2 (8-ounce) wheels brie cheese
grapes, for garnish

Combine the sugar with 1/4 cup water in a heavy-bottomed sauce-pan. Cook over medium heat until sugar dissolves. Allow the sugar mixture to boil about 8 to 10 minutes, or until it caramelizes to a golden brown.

Carefully add the butter, pecans, and salt, and stir.

Reduce the heat to low and stir in the leeks. Cook for about 1 minute, stirring frequently until the pecans are coated with a honeylike syrup. Remove from the heat and allow the pecan mixture to cool for 10 minutes.

Place the brie onto a serving dish or cheese board. Pour the pecan mixture on top of the cheese and spread it evenly to the edges. Garnish with grapes and serve with toast rounds brushed with olive oil, crackers, or sliced baguette.

Digestive cheese, and fruit there sure will bee.
—Ben Jonson, "Inviting a Friend to Supper,"
Epigrams, The Forest Underwoods, *1616*

A trip to tidewater Virginia is not complete without indulging in the renowned sweet meat of the Chesapeake blue crab. This recipe is reminiscent of the unique flavors of crab cakes that have made the region so famous.

Crabmeat Deviled Eggs "Chesapeake"

Makes 24

12 eggs
3/4 cup mayonnaise
1 tablespoon Dijon-style mustard
1 teaspoon lemon juice
1 teaspoon Worcestershire sauce
3 green onions, rinsed and chopped
    (about 2 tablespoons), divided
1 1/2 teaspoons crab or shrimp seafood
    seasoning (Old Bay)
1/2 pound crabmeat, picked clean of
    shell and cartilage
diced red bell pepper, for garnish

Gently place the eggs in a large saucepan and cover with cold water. Bring the eggs to a boil over high heat; reduce to medium-high heat and simmer the eggs for 10 minutes.

Immediately cool the eggs under cold water.

Peel the hard-cooked eggs and cut in half lengthwise. Carefully separate the yolks from the whites and place the yolks in a large bowl.

Mash the yolks together with the mayonnaise, mustard, lemon juice, Worcestershire sauce, 1 1/2 tablespoons of the green onions, and the seafood seasoning. Mix well.

Gently mix in the crabmeat to avoid breaking it up too much.

Spoon the crabmeat mixture into the egg halves and sprinkle with additional seafood seasoning, if desired. Garnish with red bell peppers and the remaining green onions, if desired, and serve chilled.

Neither better fish more plenty or variety had any of us ever seene, in any place swimming in the water, then in the bay of Chesapeack, but they are not to be caught with frying-pans.
    —*John Smith,* The Proceedings of the English Colonie
    in Virginia . . . , *1612*

Kedgeree, known as kichri in India, is a filling dish traditionally served at breakfast consisting of smoked fish, rice, and hard-cooked eggs. It is believed that a Scottish regiment in seventeenth-century India first combined smoked fish with curry. Scottish colonials introduced versions that included cream to the New World. This recipe is made with cream cheese and sour cream and makes for a hearty dip or as a comforting breakfast casserole. If the rice and the hard-cooked eggs are prepared beforehand, this recipe is very quick.

Smoked Salmon Kedgeree

Serves 8 to 12

2 tablespoons dried bread crumbs, for dusting
3 tablespoons butter, divided
1/2 cup diced onions
1 (8-ounce) package cream cheese, softened
8 ounces fresh salmon filet, cut into 1/2-inch by 1/2-inch chunks
1/4 cup dry white wine
1 cup plus 12 teaspoons sour cream, divided
8 ounces smoked salmon, chopped
1 tablespoon lemon juice
1/4 cup chopped dates
2 hard-cooked eggs, grated
1 cup cooked long-grain rice, or basmati
1 tablespoon curry powder
1/8 teaspoon cayenne pepper
2 tablespoons chopped parsley
1 teaspoon salt
1 tablespoon caviar (optional), for garnish
1/4 cup chopped fresh dill, for garnish

Preheat the oven to 350 degrees.

Lightly butter the edges of a 2-quart baking dish and dust the bottom and sides with fine bread crumbs.

Melt 2 tablespoons of the butter in a medium skillet over medium-high heat.

Add the onions and cook 3 to 5 minutes, or until softened. Transfer the onions to a large bowl.

Add the cream cheese to the warm onions and mix until smooth.

Return the skillet to the stove and melt the remaining butter over medium-high heat. Add the fresh salmon pieces. Cook the salmon, allowing it to brown, turning the pieces often.

Once the salmon is thoroughly browned, carefully pour in the wine and cover the skillet. Cook for 2 minutes, remove from the heat, and flake the salmon.

Combine the cooked salmon with the cream cheese mixture.

Add 1 cup of the sour cream and lightly mix until smooth.

Add the smoked salmon, lemon juice, dates, eggs, rice, curry powder, cayenne pepper, parsley, and salt.

Spoon the kedgeree into the baking dish. Bake for 25 minutes, or until heated through.

Garnish with the remaining sour cream, caviar, and dill, if desired, and serve warm with toast rounds and crackers. This recipe is pictured with Cheese and Chive Crisps (see page 14), Spiced Twice-Roasted Peanuts (see page 15), and Fireside Mulled Cider with Applejack (see page 125).

Cheese straws, cheese wafers, and these crisps are closely related. All that may change is the cooking time, depending on shape and size. As soon as the holidays kick off, these addictive bursts of buttery cheddar start to show up at Southern homes, usually hand delivered from friends, and always in seasonal tins carefully layered and stacked between pieces of waxed paper.

Cheese and Chive Crisps

Makes about 36

1/2 pound sharp cheddar cheese, grated
1/4 cup shredded parmesan cheese
8 tablespoons (1 stick) butter, softened
2 tablespoons chopped chives
1/8 to 1/4 teaspoon cayenne pepper
1/4 teaspoon salt
1/2 teaspoon Worcestershire sauce
1 cup all-purpose flour

Beat the cheddar cheese, parmesan cheese, butter, chives, cayenne pepper, salt, and Worcestershire sauce with an electric mixer on low speed until smooth.

Add the flour and mix with a wooden spoon just until the flour is evenly incorporated. Turn out the dough onto a lightly floured surface. Divide the dough evenly and shape by hand into two 1-inch-diameter logs. Wrap the logs in plastic and refrigerate for about 1 hour.

Preheat the oven to 375 degrees.

Slice the logs into 1/2-inch-thick disks and place them on an ungreased baking sheet. Using the back of a fork dusted with flour, gently push down on the disks to partially flatten them.

Bake for 10 to 12 minutes, or until the undersides are nicely browned.

Serve warm (see page 13) or allow the crisps to cool completely before storing them in an airtight container.

The unparalleled roasted Virginia jumbo peanut only gets better. This recipe flavors the giant goobers with barbeque seasoning from the spice section at the grocery store. Substitute any blend of spices you like: curry powder, chili powder, or even cinnamon sugar!

Spiced Twice-Roasted Peanuts

Serves 8

4 cups roasted Virginia peanuts
3 to 4 teaspoons powdered or granulated mesquite or hickory barbeque seasoning spice
¼ teaspoon cayenne pepper (optional)

Preheat the oven to 350 degrees.

Spread peanuts on a baking sheet and roast them for 5 to 8 minutes, or until the peanuts omit some of their oil.

Remove from the oven and sprinkle on the seasoning spice and cayenne pepper, if desired.

Stir the peanuts to evenly coat them with spices and return them to the oven for 2 minutes.

Season to taste with salt, if desired. Serve warm (see page 13) or allow the peanuts to cool completely before storing them in an airtight container.

It was very elegant . . . The dishes were placed all around, and there was an elegant variety of roast beef, veal, turkeys, ducks, fowls, hams, etc. puddings, jellies, oranges, apples, nuts, almonds, figs, raisins, and a variety of wines and punch.
　　　—Theophilus Bradbury, in a letter to his daughter,
　　　December 26, 1795, about dining with President and
　　　Mrs. Washington on Christmas Eve

Dressing up scraps of salty country ham with sweet relish and a touch of dry English mustard is an age-old combination of flavors long reminiscent of Williamsburg. Relishes put up in the summer and autumn were always ready for the holiday table as a condiment, side dish, or ingredient. This recipe calls for chow chow, a sweet-and-sour relish popular in the South, usually made from cabbage or green tomatoes.

Miniature Ham Relish Turnovers

Makes 18 to 20 turnovers

For the pie dough
1³/₄ cups all-purpose flour
1 teaspoon salt
8 tablespoons (1 stick) butter, frozen
¹/₂ cup ice-cold water

To make the turnovers
10 ounces lean country ham, chopped
    in a food processor
³/₄ cup chow chow, or other sweet
    relish, drained well
¹/₂ cup thinly cut green onions
¹/₄ cup chopped red bell pepper
1 tablespoon chopped parsley
1 teaspoon dry English mustard
1 egg, slightly beaten
¹/₈ teaspoon salt
chutney (optional)

Sift the flour with the salt into a large bowl.

Grate the frozen butter onto the flour mixture using a cheese grater. Distribute the butter evenly throughout the flour mixture using your hands or a pastry cutter.

Make a well in the flour mixture. Pour the water into the center of the well and mix quickly with a fork to form a soft dough. Shape the dough into a ball with your hands, wrap it in plastic, push down on the dough to form a disk, and refrigerate for at least 30 minutes.

Mix together the ham, chow chow, green onions, red bell peppers, parsley, and dry mustard in a bowl.

Roll the dough out to ¹/₈-inch thickness on a lightly floured surface. Cut into 2¹/₂- to 3-inch rounds.

Place about 2 teaspoons of the ham relish onto each round. Fold the rounds over forming half moons, press the edges together firmly, and crimp with a fork.

Preheat the oven to 450 degrees.

Mix together the egg and salt and lightly brush onto the turnovers.

Place the turnovers on ungreased baking sheets about ³/₄ inches apart and bake for 12 to 15 minutes, or until golden brown.

Serve the turnovers warm or at room temperature with a side dish of chutney, if desired.

Before sophisticated cheese making was able to take hold in the New World, the making of soft, unripened cheeses was most customary. This recipe is probably one of the tastiest, easiest, quickest, and most festive of appetizers. Colorful mixed peppercorns are usually found in the spice section at the grocery store and if you can find pink peppercorns, add more of them to the mix. Try crumbling this cheese on salads, in sandwiches, or on grilled meats.

Smoked Almond and Peppercorn Goat Cheese Log

Serves 4 to 6

½ cup smoked almonds (about 3 ounces)
2 tablespoons mixed peppercorns
½ teaspoon kosher salt
2 teaspoons chopped parsley
2 teaspoons chopped chives
2 (4-ounce) logs goat cheese
sliced green and red apples, for garnish

Coarsely chop the almonds in a food processor and place in a small bowl.

Crush the mixed peppercorns between layers of a folded kitchen towel using a meat tenderizer or other heavy implement.

Add the peppercorns to the almonds.

Mix in the salt, parsley, and chives. Spread the almond mixture on a platter.

Roll each goat cheese log in the almond mixture. Garnish with apple slices and serve with bagel crisps, toast rounds, or crackers.

'Tis not the food, but the content
That makes the Tables merriment.
        —*Robert Herrick, "Content, not cates," 1648*

Soups and Salads

Rules to be observed in Soops *or* Broths . . .
You must observe in all Broths and Soop,
that one thing does not taste more than
another; but that the Taste be equal, and
have a fine agreeable Relish, according to
what you design it for; and be sure, that
all the Greens and Herbs you put in be
cleaned washed and picked.

—Hannah Glasse, *The Art of Cookery*, 1747

No trip to Colonial Williamsburg is complete without a sampling of peanut soup at the King's Arms Tavern, which has made a tradition of serving its famous recipe. This version uses easy-to-find natural peanut butter. It is made unique with the additions of cranberry sauce and thin strips of crisp country ham, called lardoons in early American cookbooks.

Peanut Soup with Cranberry Sauce and Lardoons

Serves 4 to 6

4 tablespoons ($1/2$ stick) butter, divided
1 tablespoon peanut oil, from the top of unstirred natural peanut butter
$1/2$ cup finely chopped onions
$1/2$ cup finely chopped celery
5 tablespoons all-purpose flour
4 cups low-sodium chicken broth, or vegetable broth
4 ounces Virginia ham or salt-cured country ham, cut into thin strips
1 cup natural peanut butter
$1 1/2$ cups light cream, or half-and-half
6 heaping teaspoons whole-berry cranberry sauce
finely chopped peanuts, for garnish
parsley (optional), for garnish

Melt 3 tablespoons of the butter with the peanut oil in a 2-quart saucepan over low heat.

Add the onions and celery and cook, stirring often, 3 to 5 minutes, or until softened.

Stir in the flour and cook 2 minutes.

Pour in the broth, increase the heat to medium high, whisk until smooth, and bring to a boil, stirring constantly. Ensure that all the flour from the corners of the pan is incorporated. Reduce the heat to medium and cook, stirring often, for about 15 minutes.

Meanwhile, cook the strips of ham in the remaining butter in a medium skillet over medium-high heat for about 3 minutes, or until crisp. Allow the cooked ham strips, or lardoons, to drain on paper towels.

Pour the broth mixture into a sieve set over a large bowl and strain, pushing on the solids to extract as much liquid as possible. Discard the solids and return the broth mixture to the saucepan.

Add the peanut butter and cream to the broth mixture. Warm over low heat, whisking often until smooth, for about 5 minutes, or until hot. Do not boil.

Serve in soup bowls. Garnish with the cranberry sauce, a few lardoons, chopped peanuts, and parsley, if desired.

Gumbos, dating back to colonial times, have always included a key ingredient called filé powder, used as a thickener and flavor enhancer. Filé powder is made from the ground, dried leaves of the sassafras tree, has a woodsy flavor reminiscent of root beer, and is usually found in the spice section at the grocery store. The favored smoked Surry sausage and Chesapeake oysters transform this hearty soup into a true Virginia gumbo. For this recipe, cook the rice ahead.

Sausage and Oyster Gumbo

Serves 8 to 10

2 tablespoons butter
$1/4$ cup finely chopped onions
$1/2$ cup finely chopped green bell peppers
$1/2$ cup finely chopped celery
3 tablespoons all-purpose flour
2 cloves garlic, minced
3 cups low-sodium chicken broth
1 (10-ounce) can clam juice
3 large ripe tomatoes, peeled and chopped, or 2 (16-ounce) cans diced tomatoes with their juice
1 teaspoon dried thyme
$1/2$ teaspoon dried oregano
1 bay leaf
1 tablespoon paprika
$1/8$ teaspoon cayenne pepper
$1/2$ pound Surry sausage (or any smoked sausage) cut into $1/4$-inch-thick pieces
1 cup cut okra
$1/2$ cup chopped green onions
$1/4$ cup chopped parsley
1 pint oysters with their liquor
1 tablespoon filé powder
4 cups cooked long-grain rice

Melt the butter in a large saucepan over medium-high heat about 3 to 4 minutes, allowing it to brown.

Immediately reduce the heat to medium and add the onions, green bell peppers, and celery and cook, stirring often, 4 to 5 minutes, or until lightly browned and tender.

Stir in the flour (making a roux) and cook, stirring often, for 2 to 3 minutes, allowing it to brown.

Add the garlic and cook for 1 minute.

Whisk in the chicken broth and clam juice. Ensure that all the flour from the corners of the pan is incorporated. Increase the heat to high and whisk until smooth.

Add the tomatoes with their juice, continuing to whisk, and bring to a boil.

Reduce the heat and add the thyme, oregano, bay leaf, paprika, and cayenne pepper. Simmer the soup for 20 minutes, stirring occasionally.

Separately, cook the sausage in a large skillet over medium heat, about 4 to 5 minutes, allowing it brown, and drain away the fat.

Add the cooked sausage and okra to the soup. Return to a simmer and cook for 10 minutes.

Just prior to serving, return the soup to a boil and immediately add the green onions, parsley, and oysters with their liquor.

Remove from the heat and add the filé powder. Serve at once with warm rice.

This thick pureed soup, or pottage, of squash and pears, both ripe for the season, blend the subtle yet sweet earthy flavors of the garden and orchard. The Bartlett pear, first discovered in 1765 and known in many parts of the world as the Williams pear, grows throughout Colonial Williamsburg's Historic Area and ripens late in the season, about when the winter butternut squash is ready. It's no wonder they pair up so perfectly.

Butternut Squash and Pear Pottage

Serves 8 to 10

1 large butternut squash or 2 small ones, about 4 to 5 pounds total weight
3 tablespoons butter
3 to 4 shallots, finely chopped (about 1/2 cup)
3 to 4 ripe Bartlett pears, or Anjou, peeled, cored, and cut in 1/2-inch pieces
2 tablespoons chopped fresh ginger
4 to 5 cups low-sodium chicken broth, or vegetable broth
2 teaspoons salt
1/8 teaspoon cayenne pepper
1 cup plus 3 tablespoons heavy cream
finely diced pear (optional), for garnish
1 green onion (optional), rinsed and slivered, for garnish

To prepare the squash

Preheat the oven to 400 degrees.

Carefully cut the squash lengthwise through the middle and place the halves flat-side down on a nonstick or parchment-lined baking sheet. Pour 2 cups water into the pan and place the pan in the center of the oven with the necks of the squash toward the back of the oven.

Cook the squash for about 30 to 35 minutes, or until the middle of the neck is soft enough to indent. Once it has cooled enough to handle, peel, remove the seeds, and cut into 1-inch pieces.

For the pottage

Melt the butter in a large saucepan over medium-high heat.

Add the shallots and cook about 3 or 4 minutes, or until tender.

Add the cooked squash, pears, ginger, and 4 cups of the broth. The broth should cover the vegetables. Bring to a boil, stirring often. Reduce the heat to medium low and cook covered, stirring often, for 25 minutes.

Add the salt and cayenne pepper. Remove from the heat.

Carefully puree the soup directly in the saucepan with a stick blender, if available. Otherwise, pour the soup into a sieve set over a large bowl and strain. Place the pulp from the sieve and some of the strained soup broth in a food processor. Puree the pulp and soup broth in batches until smooth. Return the puree and soup broth to the saucepan.

Simmer over medium heat, stirring often, for 5 minutes.

Reduce the heat to low, stir in 1 cup of the cream, and adjust the seasoning to taste. Thin the pottage with milk to desired consistency.

Garnish with the remaining cream, diced pears, additional cayenne pepper, and a sliver of green onion, if desired.

This recipe highlights the historic similarities among turkey noodle soup, turkey and dumplings, and turkey potpie. In fact, in old Southern recipes it is often unclear whether "potpies" got their reference to pies from the pie-dough-like dumplings that were added while the soup was at a boil, or from the thick, creamy concoctions under a crust. Use your imagination with this soup, throwing in all sorts of holiday meal leftovers. It is best to make the noodle dough ahead.

Turkey and Homemade Noodle Dumpling Soup

Serves 10 to 12

For the noodle dough
2 cups all-purpose flour
2 tablespoons cold butter
1 egg
1/2 teaspoon salt
1/2 cup milk

For the soup
1 leftover turkey, sectioned to fit into a large saucepan
1 medium onion, chopped (about 1 cup)
1 cup chopped celery
1/2 cup chopped carrots
1 bay leaf
1/2 teaspoon thyme
1/2 teaspoon freshly ground black pepper
salt (optional)
1 cup fresh or frozen green peas
fresh thyme, for garnish

Place the flour in a large bowl. Grate the butter onto the flour and combine. Make a well in the center of the flour mixture.

Separately, mix the egg, salt, and milk together in a small bowl. Pour this liquid mixture into the center of the well and mix quickly by hand to form a soft dough. Shape the dough into a ball, wrap it in plastic, push down on the dough to form a disk, and refrigerate.

Place the turkey in a large saucepan with cold water (3 quarts, or enough to cover the turkey by 1 inch), and bring to a boil over high heat. Reduce the heat to medium and simmer, partially covered, for 1 hour.

Strain the broth and reserve. Remove all the meat from the carcass once cool enough to handle, reserve the meat, and discard the bones.

Skim the fat from the broth, return the broth to the saucepan over high heat, and bring to a boil. Reduce the heat to medium and skim any remaining fat.

Add the onions, celery, carrots, bay leaf, thyme, black pepper, and salt, if desired (salt may not be necessary if using a brine-soaked turkey). Simmer for 20 minutes, or until the carrots are tender. Reduce the heat to low and continue simmering.

Roll the noodle dough out onto a floured surface to 1/8-inch thick.

Cut the dough into 1-inch-long, 1/2-inch-wide strips using a knife or pastry cutter.

Add the reserved meat to the simmering soup and immediately begin to add the noodles and peas, stirring frequently so the noodles do not stick together. Simmer 4 to 5 minutes, garnish with fresh thyme, and serve immediately.

This classic all-American holiday recipe is the perfect relish for roast turkey, duck, ham, or just sneaked into a sandwich made of leftovers. The gelatin salad also makes a refreshing side dish dressed with a dollop of sour cream or mayonnaise. It is best to make the recipe a day ahead.

Cranberry Wreath Salad

Serves 12

1 cup dry red wine
2 (1/4-ounce) envelopes unflavored gelatin
2 (3-ounce) packages cranberry-flavored gelatin
2 cups boiling water
1/2 cup sugar
1 (12-ounce) package fresh cranberries, rinsed and patted dry
1/2 navel orange, rinsed and cut into eighths
1 (8-ounce) can crushed pineapple
1 cup halved red, seedless grapes
1 Granny Smith apple, peeled, cored, and grated
1 1/4 cups diced peaches, or 1 (16-ounce) can, drained
1/2 cup pecans (optional)
lettuce, for garnish
fresh currants, or grapes, for garnish
orange zest, for garnish

Pour the wine in a small bowl. Sprinkle the unflavored gelatin onto the wine and allow the gelatin to soften for 5 minutes.

Place the cranberry-flavored gelatin in a heat-resistant container. Separately, pour the boiling water onto the cranberry-flavored gelatin.

Immediately add the wine mixture and sugar to the gelatin mixture, stirring to dissolve. If all particles have not dissolved, heat briefly, stirring until completely dissolved.

Transfer to a medium bowl and refrigerate the gelatin for several hours or until partially set, stirring occasionally.

Finely chop the cranberries and orange pieces in a food processor using the blade attachment.

After the gelatin has partially set, add the cranberry mixture, pineapple, grapes, apples, peaches, and pecan pieces, if desired.

Spoon the wreath mixture into two 3 1/2-cup ring molds and chill until firm, preferably overnight.

Briefly place the ring molds into a shallow hot water bath and immediately invert onto round platters to unmold the wreaths. Garnish with lettuce, fresh currants or additional grapes, and orange zest.

The holly and the ivy
Are plants that are well known
Of all the trees that grow in the woods
The holly bears the crown.
—English traditional verse

The deep waters off the Virginia and North Carolina coasts provide an abundant catch of crabmeat, shrimp, and scallops. All local to the mid-Atlantic, these "fruits of the sea" are lightly marinated in a vinaigrette featuring caper berries, the brined flower buds of the caper bush. Make this salad ahead and refrigerate for several hours or marinate overnight.

"Seafruits" Salad with Caper Berry Vinaigrette

Serves 4

1 cup white wine
2 bay leaves
1 teaspoon crab or shrimp seafood seasoning (Old Bay)
4 ounces (1/4 pound) sea scallops
4 ounces (1/4 pound) shrimp, peeled and deveined
3 tablespoons capers, drained, rinsed, and roughly chopped
1 tablespoon Dijon-style mustard
1/4 cup extra-virgin olive oil
juice of 1 lemon (about 2 tablespoons)
1 tablespoon rice vinegar, or white balsamic vinegar
1 tablespoon chopped fresh tarragon leaves
1 tablespoon chopped chives
1 tablespoon chopped flat-leaf parsley
1/4 teaspoon freshly ground black pepper
1/2 pound crabmeat, picked clean of shell and cartilage
Bibb lettuce

Heat the white wine, bay leaves, and seafood seasoning in a 2-quart saucepan over high heat until it comes to a boil.

Add the scallops and shrimp and cook for 2 minutes. Strain and discard the cooking liquid. Allow the scallops and shrimp to cool.

Combine the capers, mustard, olive oil, lemon juice, vinegar, tarragon, chives, parsley, and black pepper in a medium bowl with a whisk until smooth.

Toss the cooked scallops and shrimp with the vinaigrette. Add the crabmeat and mix lightly. Allow the salad to marinate at least 30 minutes before serving. Serve chilled with Bibb lettuce.

Early Dutch settlers brought recipes for cabbage salads, called "kool sla," to the New World. The original kool sla has evolved into many kinds of exciting cole slaw recipes today. This version features fennel. During colonial times, fresh fennel bulbs were enjoyed in late summer and autumn while the seeds were collected for pickling or added to dishes for a burst of anise seasoning. Fennel is still raised in Colonial Williamsburg's Historic Area herb gardens.

Fennel Slaw with Apple Cider Cream Dressing

Serves 6

1 bulb fresh fennel
1 Granny Smith apple
2 tablespoons cider vinegar
1¹/2 cups grated green cabbage, or bok choy
¹/2 cup diced red bell pepper
3 green onions, rinsed and finely chopped (about 2 tablespoons)
¹/4 cup apple cider
¹/4 cup mayonnaise
¹/4 cup sour cream
1 teaspoon salt
cayenne pepper
Bibb lettuce

Trim any outer tough stalks and bruised areas from the fennel bulb. Trim away the hard base and discard. Trim away the feathery top, reserving some of the nicer fronds for a garnish. Slice the fennel bulb through the middle lengthwise and cut away the core. With the cut side down, slice the fennel into very thin strips.

Peel, core, and quarter the apple and grate with a cheese grater. Immediately toss the grated apples with cider vinegar to prevent browning.

Place the fennel, apple mixture, cabbage, red bell peppers, and green onions into a large bowl.

Add the apple cider, mayonnaise, sour cream, salt, and a pinch of cayenne pepper and mix well.

Serve the slaw on fresh Bibb lettuce cups and garnish with extra diced red bell peppers and reserved fennel.

The red and redest small tight heads, are best for slaw, it will not boil well, comes out black or blue, and tinges other things with which it is boiled.
—Amelia Simmons, American Cookery, 1796

Main Dishes and Hearty Casseroles

Good bread and good drink, a good fire in the hall,

brawn, pudding, and souse, and good mustard withal:

Beef, Mutton, and Pork, bread-pies of the best,

pig, veal, goose, and capon, and turkey well drest,

Cheese, apple, and nuts, jolly carols to hear,

as then in the countrey is counted good cheer.

—Thomas Tusser, "A Christmas Carrol,"
Five Hundred Points of Good Husbandry, 1577

When settlers arrived on the James River shore at Berkeley Hundred, just a few miles from current-day Williamsburg, on December 4, 1619, they proclaimed, "the day of our ship's arrival . . . shall be yearly and perpetually kept holy as a day of Thanksgiving." To the early colonists, the native turkey proved an invaluable game bird. Nowadays, serving turkey embodies the tradition of celebrating the great wealth of the harvest season. Master barbecuers know the best way of getting a crisp outer crust with the juiciest meat inside is by brining.

Roasted Brined Turkey with Pan-Drip Gravy

Serves 8 to 12

1 (12- to 14-pound) fresh or thawed
   turkey
kosher salt, for brining
brown sugar, for brining
1/2 teaspoon plus 1/4 teaspoon freshly
   ground black pepper, divided
4 tablespoons (1/2 stick) butter, melted
2 bay leaves
8 sprigs fresh thyme, or 2 teaspoons
   dried
1 lemon, quartered
1 medium onion, cut into 1/2-inch
   pieces
3 stalks celery, cut into 1/2-inch pieces
8 tablespoons all-purpose flour
fresh fruit, for garnish
sage leaves, for garnish

To brine the turkey

To save space in the refrigerator while the bird soaks, a smaller turkey is recommended. Remove the giblet bag and neck from the turkey and reserve. Rinse the turkey thoroughly under cold running water. Place the turkey in a large cooler, plastic tub, or pot.

Measuring by the gallon, add enough water to cover the turkey. Note the number of gallons. Remove the turkey.

Add enough kosher salt to the water so there is a solution of 1 cup salt for every 1 gallon water. Add 2/3 cup packed brown sugar for every 1 gallon water. For example, 3 gallons water would require 3 cups salt and 2 cups brown sugar. Mix the solution well, ensuring the salt and brown sugar dissolve.

Return the turkey and soak it at least 12 hours, ensuring the turkey stays well chilled.

For in Truth, the Turk'y is . . . [a] respectable Bird, and withal a true original Native of America . . . He is, though a little vain and silly . . . a Bird of Courage, and would not hesitate to attack a Grenadier of the British Guards, who should presume to invade his FarmYard with a red Coat on.
   —Benjamin Franklin, in a letter to his daughter, January 26, 1784

To roast the turkey

Preheat the oven to 325 degrees.

Remove the turkey from the brine and rinse thoroughly under cold running water. Pat the turkey dry and place it on a rack in a large, shallow roasting pan, breast side up.

Rub ½ teaspoon of the black pepper into the skin of the turkey.

Brush the turkey with the melted butter.

Place the bay leaves, thyme, and quartered lemon into the cavity.

Place the onions, celery, reserved giblets and neck, and 2 cups water into the pan. Cook the turkey with the legs toward the back of the oven for about 2½ hours. (For a larger turkey, be sure to adjust the roasting time accordingly.) Check the thigh meat at the thickest part using a meat thermometer. Once it reaches 180 degrees, remove the turkey from the oven. Allow the turkey to rest at least 20 minutes before carving.

For the gravy

Pour 2 cups water into the roasting pan with the turkey.

Remove the bay leaves, thyme, and quartered lemon from the cavity of the turkey and place the bay leaves and thyme into the roasting pan. Discard the quartered lemon.

Remove the turkey from the roasting pan and tent it with foil. Set the roasting pan on one or two burners set on medium-high heat. Dislodge all the pan drippings using a wooden spoon or a spatula. Allow the contents to cook for 3 minutes.

Strain the pan juices into a medium saucepan and discard the solids. Skim off excess fat from the pan juices.

Return the pan juices to a simmer over medium-high heat.

Mix the flour and 8 tablespoons water together so there are no lumps. Whisk into the simmering pan juices. Season with the remaining black pepper and simmer, stirring occasionally, for 3 to 5 minutes, or until lightly thickened.

Garnish the turkey with fresh fruit and sage leaves, and serve with the pan-drip gravy. "Bourboned" Mashed Sweet Potatoes (see page 79) and Oyster and Cracker Crumb Dressing (see page 94) are favorite side dishes.

When Columbus bumped into this continent, he was actually looking for a shortcut to the Far East's fabled Spice Islands. Spices were as valuable as silk or gold in Europe because of their preservative powers, medicinal attributes, and flavoring properties. In the sixteenth century, Westerners created a blend of mixed spices (including garam masala, coriander, and tumeric), known as curry powder, and called any dish using the blend a curry. By 1747, Hannah Glasse produced the first known modern recipe for "Currey" made "the India way." Carolina Gold rice is much like the rice grown by Southern colonists in low, marshy ground. For this recipe, the curry and the rice take about the same amount of time to cook, so start them together.

Crab and Shrimp Curry over Carolina Gold Rice Pilaf

Serves 6 to 8

For the rice pilaf

3 tablespoons butter
1 cinnamon stick
1 1/2 cups Carolina Gold rice, or
   basmati, rinsed
3 cups hot water
3 tablespoons dried currants
1 teaspoon salt
3 tablespoons chopped green onions

Melt the butter in a medium saucepan over medium-high heat. Add the cinnamon stick and cook in the butter for 2 to 3 minutes. Add the rice and stir so all the rice is coated with the butter.

Add the water, currants, and salt. Increase the heat to high and bring to a boil. Stir and reduce the heat to medium low and cover. Cook for about 20 minutes, or until all the liquid is absorbed.

Fluff the rice with a fork, stir in the green onions, transfer the rice to a bowl, and keep warm.

What will not Lux'ry taste? Earth, Sea, and Air
Are daily ransack'd for the Bill of Fare.
   —John Gay, Trivia, 1716

For the curry

4 tablespoons (1/2 stick) butter
1 large onion, chopped (about 1 1/2 cups)
3 cloves garlic, minced (about 1 1/2 tablespoons)
1 tablespoon minced fresh ginger
2 apples, peeled, cored, and diced (about 1 1/2 cups)
3 tablespoons curry powder
1/8 teaspoon cayenne pepper
1 tablespoon cornstarch
1 cup heavy cream
1 (14-ounce) can unsweetened coconut milk
1 pound shrimp, peeled and deveined
1 pound crabmeat, picked clean of shell and cartilage
1/2 teaspoon salt
1/2 pound mussels (optional) debearded, rinsed, and cooked (available frozen)
1/2 cup grated coconut, toasted for garnish
1 green onion, rinsed and chopped, for garnish
fruit chutney (optional)

Melt the butter in a large saucepan over medium-high heat. Add the onions and cook 3 to 5 minutes, or until soft.

Add the garlic, ginger, and apples and cook for 2 to 3 minutes.

Add the curry powder and cayenne pepper. Stir together until evenly mixed.

Dissolve the cornstarch in the heavy cream and stir into the curry mixture.

Pour in the coconut milk and stir. Increase the heat to high, stirring constantly, and bring to boil.

Immediately add the shrimp and return to a simmer. Reduce the heat to medium high and cook for 3 minutes.

Add the crabmeat and cook for an additional 3 minutes, or until thoroughly heated.

Season with salt, to taste.

Add the mussels, if desired, or heat them separately.

Garnish this dish with the grated coconut and green onions and serve it with a tangy fruit chutney.

Prime Rib! After the brief and hurried Thanksgiving weekend has passed, and with it the turkey, trimmings, leftover sandwiches, and turkey soup, most households begin to crave other holiday flavors. This standing rib of beef is famously accompanied by Yorkshire pudding.

Rosemary-Rubbed Standing Rib of Beef

Serves 8

3 tablespoons chopped fresh rosemary, or 2 tablespoons dried
2 tablespoons minced dried onion
2 tablespoons minced dried garlic
2 tablespoons kosher salt
2 teaspoons freshly ground black pepper
2 tablespoons extra-virgin olive oil
1 (10- to 12- pound) beef rib roast with bones (note the weight to approximate the cooking time)
1 medium onion, cut into eighths
3 carrots, peeled and cut into 1/2-inch disks
3 celery stalks, cut into 1/2-inch pieces
2 cups beef stock, or low-sodium beef broth
fresh rosemary sprigs, for garnish

Preheat the oven to 450 degrees.

Combine the rosemary, dried onion, garlic, salt, black pepper, and olive oil in a small bowl. Place the rib roast into a large roasting pan. Rub all sides of the rib roast with the rosemary mixture.

Place the onions, carrots, and celery under and around the rib roast. Be sure the rib roast is bone side down.

Pour 1 cup water into the roasting pan and place it on the bottom rack of the oven. Immediately reduce the heat to 350 degrees. Estimate the cooking time as 12 to 15 minutes per pound for a rare rib roast.

After 1 hour, carefully pour 1 cup water into the roasting pan.

After about 1 hour, check for doneness with a meat thermometer in the center of the roast. Roast to 130 degrees for rare, 140 degrees for medium, and 160 degrees for well done. Place the rib roast on a carving board with a drip trough and tent it with foil. Allow the rib roast to rest about 20 minutes before slicing.

Place the roasting pan on the stove over one or two burners set on medium heat. Add the beef stock and dislodge all the pan drippings using a wooden spoon or spatula. Strain the beef stock into a medium saucepan, reserving the vegetables. Return the beef stock to a simmer over medium-high heat.

Skim off the excess fat, adjust the seasoning to taste, and keep hot.

Serve the standing rib of beef with the reserved vegetables, the sauce, and Buttery Yorkshire Pudding (see page 80), and garnish with sprigs of fresh rosemary.

When mighty roast Beef was the Englishman's Food,
It ennobled our Hearts, and enriched our Blood,
Our soldiers were brave and our Courtiers were good.
Oh! the roast Beef of England.
—Henry Fielding, The Grub-Street Opera, 1731

The Chesapeake Bay is abundant with flounder as they spawn in the more shallow waters from late summer through midwinter. Hard-shell clams, however, prefer the saltier waters of the open bay and Atlantic ocean. Together these local delicacies harmonize the treasured seafood flavors of the tidewater region.

Clam-Stuffed Flounder with Thyme Butter

Serves 6

For the clam stuffing

3 tablespoons butter

1 medium onion, finely chopped
(about 1 cup)

1/2 cup diced red bell peppers, or
pimentos

2 (5-ounce) cans chopped clams, or
baby clams, drained, reserving the
juice (for the flounder recipe)

2 teaspoons Dijon-style mustard

1 tablespoon Worcestershire sauce

juice of 1 lemon (about 2 tablespoons)

2 tablespoons chopped parsley

3/4 teaspoon salt

1/2 teaspoon freshly ground black
pepper

1 cup fresh bread crumbs (about
4 slices)

For the flounder

6 (6-ounce) flounder filets

1/2 teaspoon salt

1/4 teaspoon freshly ground black
pepper

1/2 cup dry white wine

8 sprigs fresh thyme, or 1/2 teaspoon
dried

reserved clam juice (from the clam
stuffing recipe)

1 tablespoon butter

Melt the butter in a large saucepan over medium heat.

Add the onions and cook, stirring for 3 to 4 minutes, or until softened.

Stir in the red bell peppers and cook for 1 minute.

Add the clams, mustard, Worcestershire sauce, lemon juice, parsley, and salt. Cook for 4 to 5 minutes, stirring often, or until the mixture is heated through.

Remove from the heat, season with the black pepper, and stir in the bread crumbs.

———————

Preheat the oven to 375 degrees and butter a 2-quart baking dish.

If the fish filets are somewhat thick and are not flexible enough to roll, place the filets between two layers of plastic and gently tap with a mallet, tenderizing the filets until more pliable.

Season the filets with the salt and black pepper and, with the skin side of the fish up, spread each filet with 4 tablespoons clam stuffing.

Roll up each filet beginning at the widest end to form a tube shape. Cut down through the center of the filet three-fourths of the way with a sharp knife. Turn under each end of the filet so the center is facing up, forming a partial spiral. Place each filet in the baking dish cut-side up. Pour in the white wine and add the thyme.

Cover the fish with a layer of parchment or waxed paper and then cover the baking dish with aluminum foil.

Bake for about 20 minutes, or until the fish is firm in the center.

Place the fish on a serving platter and keep warm.

Strain the juices into a small saucepan, add the reserved clam juice, and reduce the juices by half over high heat.

Remove from the stove and whisk in the butter.

Serve the sauce with the flounder and garnish with lemon slices and additional sprigs of thyme.

In this recipe, the genuine flavors of the prized cut of beef remain distinctive. Roast tenderloin is suitable for any elegant holiday fest. The sauce borrows the classic combination of flavors from sauce béarnaise and is quick and easy. Make the sauce ahead and serve it slightly chilled.

Peppery Roast Tenderloin of Beef with Tarragon Sauce

Serves 6 to 8

For the sauce
2 tablespoons dried tarragon
1 to 2 shallots, chopped (about 2 tablespoons)
1/2 cup tarragon vinegar, or red wine vinegar
1 small potato, peeled, boiled, mashed, and chilled (about 2 tablespoons)
3/4 cup mayonnaise
2 tablespoons extra-virgin olive oil

For the tenderloin
2 1/2 to 3 pounds beef tenderloin, trimmed of excess fat and silverskin completely removed
1 teaspoon kosher salt
2 teaspoons coarsely ground black pepper

Combine the tarragon, shallots, and vinegar in a small saucepan over medium heat. Increase the heat to high and bring to a boil. Return the heat to medium and cook 10 and 12 minutes, or until the tarragon mixture is reduced to nearly dry. Transfer the tarragon mixture to a bowl and refrigerate for about 20 minutes.

Place the tarragon mixture, potato, and mayonnaise into a food processor with the blade attachment. Pulse and then puree. Drizzle in the olive oil with the food processor running.

Remove the sauce from the food processor, season to taste with salt and black pepper, and refrigerate.

Preheat the oven to 400 degrees and rub the tenderloin with the salt and black pepper.

Sear the tenderloin on an outdoor grill or in a large skillet with 1 tablespoon vegetable oil over high heat 4 to 5 minutes, or until well browned.

Transfer the tenderloin to a medium roasting pan. Add 1/2 cup water to the roasting pan and place the tenderloin in the middle of the oven.

Immediately reduce the heat to 350 degrees. Roast the tenderloin for about 25 to 30 minutes, carefully turning it over one time. Roast the tenderloin until a meat thermometer reads 120 degrees for rare or 130 degrees for medium rare.

Allow the tenderloin to rest for 5 minutes. Serve with the tarragon sauce. Herbed Cherry Tomatoes with Black Olives (see page 75), Braised Romaine with Brown Butter and Fennel Seeds (see page 76), Buttermilk Mashed Rutabagas (see page 78), and Sweet Potato Raisin Bread (see page 92) accompany the tenderloin.

Game hens are the perfect choice for a more intimate holiday dinner, especially when they are trimmed with your favorite stuffing or dressing. Better yet, there should be enough for leftovers. Brandying peaches is a time-honored method of preserving these fruits of summer and are usually available at the grocery store. If you cannot find the real thing, use fresh, ripe peaches or good-quality frozen peach slices with a healthy splash of brandy. In this recipe, the peaches are added at the end to ensure the warming brandy content does not evaporate.

Holiday-Dressed Game Hens and Brandied Peaches

Serves 2

2 (18- to 20-ounce) games hens
1/2 teaspoon salt
1/4 teaspoon freshly ground black
    pepper
1 tablespoon extra-virgin olive oil
1/2 lemon, cut into halves
1/2 cup low-sodium chicken broth
3 to 4 brandied peaches, pitted and
    quartered with their juice
1 tablespoon butter

Preheat the oven to 425 degrees.

Rinse the game hens thoroughly under cold running water and pat dry.

Combine the salt and black pepper in a small dish. Rub the salt and pepper mixture into the inside and outside of the game hens and brush with the olive oil. Tuck the wing tips back and place the game hens on a rack inside a small roasting pan.

Place the lemon halves into the cavity of each game hen.

Roast the game hens for 50 to 60 minutes, or until juices from the thickest part of the thigh run clear when pierced. Midway through the cooking time, begin making the stuffing or dressing.

Remove the game hens from the roasting pan and allow them to rest for 5 minutes before serving. Place the roasting pan on the stove over one of the burners set on medium heat.

Add the chicken broth and dislodge all the pan drippings using a wooden spoon or spatula and bring to a boil. Strain the pan juices into a medium saucepan and simmer over medium-high heat for 2 to 3 minutes. Skim off any excess fat.

Add the peaches and cook for 1 minute.

Turn the stove off and whisk in the butter. Adjust the seasoning to taste.

Serve with the brandied peaches. These game hens are delicious served with Pan-Seared Cucumbers with Dill and Buttered Pecans (see page 72) and Corn Bread, Mushroom, and Chestnut Stuffing (see page 93).

The classic compote of stewed pears cooked down with red cabbage makes a wonderful sweet-and-sour accompaniment to this crispy pork preparation. Make the cabbage first, since it only gets better as it stews.

Sugar-and-Spice Crusted Pork Tenderloin with Cabbage and Pear Compote

Serves 6 to 8

For the compote
1 1/2 pounds red cabbage, cut in thin strips (about 6 cups)
3 fresh pears, peeled, cored, and diced into 1/2-inch pieces (about 3 cups)
2 tablespoons extra-virgin olive oil
1 cinnamon stick
2 teaspoons salt
1/4 cup rice vinegar

Combine the red cabbage, pears, olive oil, cinnamon stick, salt, and rice vinegar with 1/2 cup water in a nonreactive saucepan over medium heat. Cover and stir occasionally. Cook for 45 to 60 minutes, or until the cabbage is tender.

For the pork tenderloin
2 1/2 pounds boneless pork tenderloin
4 tablespoon Dijon-style mustard
2 teaspoons kosher salt
1 tablespoon coarsely ground or cracked black pepper
2 tablespoons light brown sugar
1 teaspoon dried minced garlic
1 teaspoon dried minced onion
1 teaspoon rubbed dried sage
1 teaspoon dried thyme
1/2 cup dried bread crumbs
1 tablespoon extra-virgin olive oil
fresh sage, for garnish

Preheat the oven to 475 degrees.

Place the pork tenderloin on a large platter or baking sheet and coat with the mustard.

Separately, mix together the kosher salt, black pepper, light brown sugar, garlic, onion, sage, thyme, and bread crumbs in a small bowl.

Place the bread crumb mixture on a separate platter or baking sheet. Firmly roll the pork tenderloin into the bread crumb mixture, ensuring the pork tenderloin is evenly coated.

Oil the bottom of a shallow, medium roasting pan with the olive oil. Place the pork tenderloin in the center of the roasting pan.

Roast for 20 minutes, then reduce the heat to 350 degrees, and roast for another 10 to 15 minutes, or until a meat thermometer reads 145 to 150 degrees.

Remove the pork tenderloin from the oven. Allow it to rest for 5 minutes before slicing. Garnish with fresh sage and serve with the cabbage and pear compote. Black-Eyed Peas with Grilled Red Onion Pickle (see page 81) and Skillet-Baked Corn Bread (see page 90) round out this meal.

The age-old method of stewing meats in a cream sauce made rich and thick with egg yolks, called fricassee, dates to sixteenth-century France. Martha Washington had a recipe handed down to her from her family TO MAKE A FRYKACY OF CHIKIN LAMB VEALE OR RABBITS. Susannah Carter dedicates an entire chapter to fricassees in The Frugal Colonial Housewife. In Mary Randolph's early American cookbook, she lists a recipe she called TO FRICASSEE COD SOUNDS AND TONGUES. This version features oysters, always abundant in tidewater Virginia.

Oyster Fricassee

Serves 6 to 8

12 tablespoons (1½ sticks) butter, divided
2 medium onions, chopped (about 1½ cups)
1½ cups chopped celery
8 tablespoons all-purpose flour
2 cups light cream, or half-and-half
2 teaspoons salt
⅛ teaspoon cayenne pepper
¼ teaspoon freshly ground black pepper
1 teaspoon fresh thyme, or ½ teaspoon dried
2 teaspoons chopped parsley
1 quart shucked oysters, drained, reserving the oyster liquor
4 egg yolks
48 round buttery crackers, crumbled
lemon slices, for garnish
fresh thyme, for garnish

Melt 8 tablespoons of the butter in a medium saucepan over medium heat.

Add the onions and celery and cook about 3 to 5 minutes, or until softened.

Stir in the flour (making a roux) and cook, stirring frequently, for 2 to 3 minutes.

Whisk in the cream. Ensure that all the flour from the corners of the pan is incorporated. Increase the heat to medium high, whisk until smooth, and bring to a simmer, creating a cream sauce.

Reduce the heat to medium and add the salt, cayenne pepper, black pepper, thyme, parsley, and reserved oyster liquor. Stir until smooth and remove from the stove.

Gradually whisk in the egg yolks, stirring to ensure they do not scramble.

Preheat the oven to 400 degrees and butter a 4-quart baking dish (or individual casserole dishes).

Pour half the cream sauce into the baking dish.

Evenly distribute half the oysters on top of the cream sauce.

Sprinkle half the cracker crumbs on the oysters.

Pour the remaining cream sauce onto the cracker crumbs; evenly distribute the remaining oysters on top of the cream sauce; and sprinkle the remaining cracker crumbs on the oysters.

Melt the remaining butter and drizzle on top of the cracker crumbs.

Bake for 25 to 30 minutes, or until the sauce is set like custard.

Garnish with lemon slices and additional sprigs of thyme and serve with a light salad.

In late fall and early winter, colonial Virginians were blessed with an abundance of waterfowl migrating over the Chesapeake Bay via the Atlantic flyway. Duck hunting is a cherished tradition in the vast wetlands of tidewater Virginia. Duck and seasonal kumquats, with their sweet outer peel and slightly tart sour flesh, is a classic combination. In this recipe, figs add a concentrated fruit flavor while naturally thickening the sauce. Introduced to the Americas by European settlers, figs flourished in colonial gardens. Today, fig trees thrive in Williamsburg.

Roasted Whole Duck with Braised Kumquats and Figs

Serves 2 to 4

1 (5- to 6-pound) duck, thawed
1 teaspoon salt
1/2 teaspoon freshly ground black pepper
1/2 lemon, cut into thirds
4 sprigs fresh thyme, or 1 teaspoon dried
1 medium onion, sliced
12 kumquats, halved, or 1 orange, cut into eighths
6 ounces dried black mission figs, destemmed and halved (about 1 cup)
1/2 cup low-sodium soy sauce
1 tablespoon butter

Preheat the oven to 400 degrees.

Remove the neck and livers from the cavity of the duck. Trim away excess fat from the neck and tail of the duck. Rinse the duck thoroughly under cold running water and pat dry.

Combine the salt and black pepper in a small dish. Rub the salt and pepper mixture into the inside and outside of the duck. Tuck the wing tips back and place the duck on a rack inside a medium roasting pan.

Fill the cavity of the duck with the lemon pieces and thyme.

Place the onions and 1 cup water into the roasting pan. Roast the duck with the legs toward the back of the oven.

After 1 hour, carefully add the kumquats and figs to the roasting pan. Reduce the heat to 350 degrees and cook the duck for an additional 40 minutes, or until the internal temperature of the thigh is 180 degrees.

Remove the duck from the roasting pan and tent it with foil. Allow it to rest 15 to 20 minutes before carving.

Carefully add 1 1/2 cups water to the roasting pan. Dislodge all the pan drippings using a wooden spoon or spatula.

Carefully strain the pan juices into a medium saucepan, reserving the onions, kumquats, and figs. Skim off excess fat from the pan juices.

Return the pan juices to a simmer over medium heat. Add the reserved onions, kumquats, and figs to the saucepan. Add the soy sauce and simmer for 10 minutes.

Remove the saucepan from the stove and whisk in the butter.

Present the duck whole and serve with the braised fruit sauce and Wild Rice Stuffing with Toasted Pine Nuts and Dates (see page 95).

In colonial times, venison was the most prized addition to the harvest and winter tables. Jerusalem artichokes are actually part of the sunflower family and native to North America. The short, fleshy stems, when left unpeeled, lend a delicate, nutty flavor to this classic rendition.

Venison Stew with Jerusalem Artichokes

Serves 10 to 12

2¹/₂ pounds venison stew meat, cut into 1-inch pieces

2 teaspoons salt

2 tablespoons vegetable oil

2 medium, sweet onions, cut into ¹/₂-inch pieces

8 ounces medium mushrooms, quartered (about 1¹/₂ cups)

1 cup dry red wine

3 medium carrots, peeled and cut into ¹/₂-inch rounds

3 stalks celery, cut into ¹/₂-inch pieces

2 medium white turnips, peeled and cut into ¹/₂-inch pieces

1 tablespoon chopped garlic

4¹/₂ cups low-sodium beef broth, divided

1 (14-ounce) can diced tomatoes with their juices

12 ounces Jerusalem artichokes, scrubbed and cut into ¹/₂-inch pieces

1 teaspoon fresh thyme, or ¹/₂ teaspoon dried

2 bay leaves

¹/₂ teaspoon freshly ground black pepper

1 tablespoon coarsely ground or chopped juniper berries

2 tablespoons all-purpose flour

¹/₄ cup lingonberry preserves, or whole-berry cranberry sauce

Season the venison with the salt.

Brown the venison in the vegetable oil in a large skillet over high heat. Be sure to brown the venison evenly on all sides, perhaps in batches. Do not crowd the pan.

Lift the venison out of the skillet and transfer it to a small bowl.

Add the onions and mushrooms to the skillet and reduce the heat to medium high. Cook, stirring occasionally, for 4 to 5 minutes, or until well browned.

Add the red wine and cook for 1 minute.

Combine the venison and mushroom mixture with the carrots, celery, turnips, garlic, 4 cups of the broth, and the tomatoes with their juices in a large saucepan over high heat. Bring to a boil, reduce to low heat, and simmer for 15 minutes.

Add the Jerusalem artichokes, thyme, bay leaves, and black pepper to the saucepan. Return to a simmer and cook for 45 minutes, or until the venison is tender.

Add the juniper berries.

Mix the flour with the remaining broth, ensuring there are no lumps. Stir the flour mixture into the stew.

Return the stew to a simmer and cook for 10 minutes.

Just prior to serving, stir in the lingonberry preserves. Serve piping hot with Skillet-Baked Corn Bread (see page 90) and rice.

This recipe is a perfect breakfast or luncheon casserole filled with all things wonderful about the Old Dominion. Smokehouse sausage from the south side of the James River, indigenous squash, and Shenandoah apples meet under a crunchy, crumbly topping. Look for cooking apples such as Stayman, Winesap, York, or Granny Smith.

Surry Sausage, Squash, and Apple Bake with Savory Strudel Topping

Serves 6

1 pound cooked Surry sausage, or kielbasa

2 medium zucchini, cut in small disks

2 yellow squash, cut in small disks

1½ cups peeled and thinly sliced butternut squash

4 medium apples, peeled, cored, and sliced into eighths

1½ cups grated cheddar cheese

1 teaspoon salt

½ teaspoon freshly ground black pepper

1 tablespoon extra-virgin olive oil

2 hard-cooked eggs, peeled and grated

2 tablespoons chopped parsley

½ teaspoon salt

¼ teaspoon freshly ground black pepper

2 cups dried bread crumbs

4 tablespoons (½ stick) butter, cold and grated

Preheat the oven to 350 degrees and butter a 2-quart baking dish. Cut the sausage into small disks.

Place the sausage, zucchini, yellow squash, butternut squash, apples, and cheddar cheese in a large bowl. Season with the salt and black pepper and mix together.

Place the mixture into the baking dish, drizzle with the olive oil, and begin baking the casserole.

Meanwhile, combine the eggs, parsley, salt, and black pepper in a medium bowl.

Combine the bread crumbs with the cold butter in a food processor with the blade attachment. Briefly chop the butter into the bread crumbs using the pulse feature.

Mix together the bread crumb mixture with the grated egg mixture in the medium bowl. Cover and refrigerate.

After the casserole has cooked for 30 minutes, remove it from the oven and sprinkle the savory strudel topping evenly on top of the casserole. Bake for 60 additional minutes, or until the apples are tender.

This recipe is pictured with freshly squeezed orange juice and freshly baked Applesauce Buttermilk Biscuits (see page 89).

From the moment ships arrived in nearby Jamestown in 1607, a rich tradition of pork in Virginia was born. The climate and forage allowed the hogs to flourish. It is said that the hogs' diet of peanuts combined with salt curing and old hickory smokehouses makes the delectable Virginia hams world famous. Ham loaf is a wonderful and inexpensive way to use leftovers, but after making it once, you may find yourself shopping specifically for this recipe.

Country Ham Loaf with Dried Cherry Sauce

Serves 6 to 8

For the ham loaf
1 tablespoon butter
1 medium onion, finely chopped (about 1 cup)
1 1/2 pounds ground fresh pork
1 pound ground sugar-cured smoked ham
1/2 pound ground Virginia country ham
1 egg
3/4 cup buttermilk
3 tablespoons Dijon-style mustard
2 tablespoons chopped parsley
1/2 teaspoon freshly ground black pepper
1/2 cup fresh bread crumbs (about 2 slices bread)

For the dried cherry sauce
2 tablespoons butter
3 to 4 shallots, chopped (about 1/2 cup)
1 1/2 tablespoons all-purpose flour
1 cup dry red wine
1 cup ruby port wine
1 cup low-sodium chicken broth
1 bay leaf
3/4 cup dried cherries

Preheat the oven to 375 degrees.

Melt the butter in a skillet over medium heat and cook the onions 3 to 5 minutes, or until soft. Allow to cool.

Place the pork, smoked ham, and country ham in a large bowl. Add the cooked onions.

Whisk together the egg, buttermilk, mustard, parsley, and black pepper in a small bowl.

Briefly mix the egg mixture and bread crumbs into the meat mixture. Do not over mix. Form the meat mixture into loaf and place the loaf on a lightly buttered or parchment-lined baking sheet. Bake for 1 hour, or until a meat thermometer reads 170 degrees.

———————

Melt the butter in a medium saucepan over medium heat.

Add the shallots and cook, stirring often, 3 to 4 minutes, or until softened.

Stir in the flour (making a roux) using a wooden spoon. Cook for 2 minutes, stirring frequently.

Carefully whisk in the red wine, port wine, and broth. Increase the heat to medium high and bring to a boil. Ensure that all the flour from the corners of the pan is incorporated.

Add the bay leaf and cherries and reduce the heat to low. Cook the sauce over low heat, stirring occasionally, about 25 minutes, or until the sauce has reduced to 2 cups.

Remove the bay leaf and season with salt and black pepper to taste. Keep warm.

Garnish the ham loaf with fresh herbs and serve it with the dried cherry sauce and Stewed Cabbage with Tarragon and Leeks (see page 73).

This hearty combination of autumnal and winter vegetables is a wonderful main dish. Many types of catsups were common in early American cookbooks, including mushroom, walnut, oyster, and mussel. This variation uses the entire mushroom in a pureed state as opposed to eighteenth-century recipes, which called for straining the mushrooms. Make the catsup a day ahead. Also, start the wild rice about an hour before serving, since it takes extra time to cook.

Vegetable-Stuffed Acorn Squash with Wild Rice and Mushroom Catsup

Serves 4

For the mushroom catsup
1 (8-ounce) package button or crimini
  mushrooms, rinsed and quartered
6 cloves garlic, peeled
$1/4$ cup chopped red bell pepper
$1/2$ teaspoon salt
$1/8$ teaspoon mace, or ground nutmeg
$1/8$ teaspoon allspice
1 teaspoon sugar
cayenne pepper
1 teaspoon red wine vinegar
1 cup dry white wine
1 tablespoon extra-virgin olive oil

Puree the mushrooms, garlic, red bell pepper, salt, mace, allspice, sugar, cayenne pepper, red wine vinegar, white wine, and olive oil in a food processor with the blade attachment. Add some water, if necessary, to ensure the ingredients mix smoothly.

Place the mushroom puree into a heavy-bottomed saucepan and cook over medium heat for 25 to 30 minutes, or until the catsup is reduced by half.

Allow the catsup to cool and transfer it to a dressing bottle or condiment jar. Refrigerate; shake before using.

For I look upon it, that he who does not mind his belly,
will hardly mind any thing else.
                          —Samuel Johnson, 1763

For the stuffed squash

1/2 cup wild rice, rinsed

1 bay leaf

2 large acorn squash

4 teaspoons plus 2 tablespoons butter, divided

2 tablespoons light brown sugar

1 tablespoon extra-virgin olive oil

1 cup peeled and cubed sweet potatoes

1 cup pearl onions

1 cup peeled, cored, and cubed Granny Smith apples

1/2 cup dried cranberries

2 small yellow squash, cubed (about 1 cup)

2 cups chopped fresh spinach

1/4 teaspoon dried thyme

1/4 teaspoon dried ginger

1/2 teaspoon salt

1/4 teaspoon freshly ground black pepper

1/3 cup slivered almonds, toasted (about 2 ounces)

To prepare the wild rice

Place the wild rice, bay leaf, and 2 cups water in a heavy, small saucepan over high heat. Bring to a boil. Reduce the heat to low. Partially cover the saucepan and cook the wild rice for 50 to 60 minutes, or until the wild rice has puffed.

Remove the wild rice from the stove and cover the saucepan tightly. Allow the wild rice to rest for 10 minutes.

Drain off excess water and set the wild rice aside.

To prepare the squash

Preheat the oven to 375 degrees.

Cut the acorn squash in half and trim the bases so they stand evenly on their ends.

Scoop out the seeds and place 1 teaspoon of butter into each squash half.

Sprinkle the inside and rim of each squash half with some salt and the light brown sugar.

Set the squash halves into a shallow, large roasting pan.

Pour 1 cup water into the roasting pan and bake the squash in the oven for 45 to 50 minutes, or until they are just soft. Occasionally baste the edges of the squash with the buttery-brown sugar from inside the squash. Remove from the oven and keep the squash covered in a warm place.

For the vegetable stuffing

Melt 1 tablespoon of the butter with the olive oil in a large skillet over medium heat.

Add the sweet potatoes and cover. Stir the sweet potato mixture occasionally and allow to cook about 5 to 6 minutes, or until tender.

Turn the heat up to high and add the pearl onions, apples, and cranberries, and cook 3 to 4 minutes, or until the pearl onions are tender.

Add the yellow squash and spinach. Stir and cook for 3 to 4 minutes.

Add the remaining butter and the thyme and ginger.

Cook for 2 minutes and add 1 1/2 cups cooked wild rice.

Season with the salt and black pepper and heat thoroughly.

Place the vegetable stuffing into the warm acorn squash and sprinkle with toasted almonds. Serve with the mushroom catsup.

Vegetables and Side Dishes

Christmas dinner . . . cabbage pudding,

Colliflowers, artichoakes, cheese-cakes,

gooseberry tarts jellys, creems, raisons,

grapes, nuts, almonds, apples &c &c.

—Martha Blodget, Christmas 1796

Spoon breads and savory puddings were popular in England through the ages. When English settlers first arrived in the New World, American Indians introduced them to "mahiz," a native grain now called maize. It is no wonder that the settlers immediately incorporated corn into their time-honored pudding preparations. This recipe includes green and red bell peppers to dress up the corn pudding for Christmas.

Christmas Corn Pudding

Serves 6

1/2 cup stone-ground yellow cornmeal
2 cups milk
2 tablespoons butter, melted
16 ounces fresh sweet corn, or frozen corn, thawed
2 tablespoons all-purpose flour
2 teaspoons salt
1 teaspoon sugar
1/3 cup finely chopped green bell pepper
1/3 cup finely chopped red bell pepper
4 eggs, beaten
fresh parsley, for garnish

Preheat the oven to 350 degrees and butter a 1-quart baking dish.

Place the cornmeal into a medium bowl.

Place the milk with the butter in a medium saucepan over medium-high heat and bring to a simmer.

Stir the hot milk mixture into the cornmeal and allow to set for 3 minutes, forming a cornmeal mush.

Combine the corn, flour, salt, and sugar in a medium bowl. Stir the corn mixture just until the flour is distributed evenly.

Add the green bell peppers and red bell peppers, and mix.

Mix together the corn mixture with the cornmeal mush.

Mix in the eggs and pour into the baking dish. Place the baking dish inside a larger baking dish. Pour hot water into the outer baking dish and bake for 45 to 50 minutes, or until the corn pudding is firm in the center.

Garnish with a sprig of fresh parsley.

Finding a fresh green vegetable during the winter holidays can be expensive and sometimes difficult. If you have never had a cucumber browned in a hot skillet, you are in for a pleasant surprise. The pecans, native to the South, add a nutty crunch.

Pan-Seared Cucumbers with Dill and Buttered Pecans

Serves 6

6 cucumbers, rinsed and partially
   peeled, retaining some of the green
1/2 teaspoon salt
1/4 teaspoon freshly ground black
   pepper
2 tablespoons extra-virgin olive oil
2 tablespoons chopped fresh dill
2 tablespoons butter
1 cup pecan pieces (about 8 ounces)

Cut the cucumbers through the center lengthwise. Remove the seeds and cut the cucumbers into 3/4-inch pieces. Sprinkle with the salt and black pepper.

Heat the olive oil in a large skillet over medium-high heat. Increase the heat to high and add the cucumbers.

Cook the cucumbers for 2 to 3 minutes, stirring occasionally, or until lightly browned.

Stir in the dill and remove from the heat. Place the cucumbers in a serving bowl and keep warm.

Melt the butter in the same skillet over medium-high heat.

Add the pecans when the butter begins to foam and turns light brown. Cook for 1 minute, or until the pecans are thoroughly heated. Season with a pinch of salt.

Pour the pecans over the cucumbers and serve (see page 51).

Cucumbers, are of many kinds; the prickly is best for pickles, but generally bitter; the white is difficult to raise and tender; chose the bright green, smooth and proper sized.
   —*Amelia Simmons, American Cookery, 1796*

Cabbage kept well in colonial gardens through the first frost and embellished many a winter table. This seasonally appropriate side dish complements any meal. Adding pork chops or smoked ham transforms this recipe into true comfort food, making for a good winter brunch or dinner. This easiest of preparations is made the old-fashioned way and served in its own "pot likker," or broth.

Stewed Cabbage with Tarragon and Leeks

Serves 4 to 6

1 large head cabbage, cored and cut
  into 1-inch pieces
3 medium potatoes, peeled and grated
  (about 2½ cups)
2 leeks, most of the green top discarded,
  cut in ½-inch pieces and rinsed well
  (about 1½ cups)
1 cup apple juice
½ cup tarragon vinegar
2 tablespoons butter
1 tablespoon chopped fresh tarragon, or
  1 heaping teaspoon dried
1 teaspoon sugar
2 teaspoons salt
½ teaspoon freshly ground black pepper
fresh tarragon, for garnish

Combine the cabbage, potatoes, leeks, apple juice, tarragon vinegar, butter, tarragon, sugar, salt, and black pepper with ½ cup water in a large, nonreactive saucepan over medium-high heat, and cover. Cook for 20 minutes, stirring occasionally.

Reduce the heat to medium low and cover. Cook for an additional 20 to 30 minutes, or until the cabbage is tender.

Garnish with additional chopped fresh tarragon (see page 63).

This delicious little side dish of tomatoes features Herbs de Provence, a blend of lavender, basil, rosemary, thyme, savory, and other herbs. According to legend, lavender gets its aromatic scent from when the Virgin Mary dried baby Jesus' swaddling clothes on a bed of wild lavender. In the eighteenth century the tomato, a member of the nightshade family, was often considered harmful to eat. Colonial physician John de Sequeyra is credited with introducing the tomato into Williamsburg's kitchens about the time of the Revolution. Today you can garnish a roast tenderloin or the holiday turkey with these bite-size bursts of flavor.

Herbed Cherry Tomatoes with Black Olives

Serves 6 to 8

2 pints cherry tomatoes, stems removed
   and rinsed
2 tablespoons extra-virgin olive oil
3 tablespoons pitted and chopped
   kalamata olives, or niçoise
1/4 teaspoon salt
1/8 teaspoon freshly ground black
   pepper
1 tablespoon Herbs de Provence
2 tablespoons dried bread crumbs
1 tablespoon chopped parsley
fresh parsley sprig, for garnish

Combine the tomatoes with the olive oil in a large skillet over medium heat. Add the olives, salt, black pepper, and Herbs de Provence. Heat for about 5 minutes, stirring occasionally, just until the tomatoes are warm.

Sprinkle in the bread crumbs and parsley and heat for 1 minute. Garnish with a sprig of parsley and serve immediately.

*Yet shall you have to rectifie your palate,
An olive, capers, or some better sallade.*
   —Ben Jonson, "Inviting a Friend to Supper,"
Epigrams, The Forest Underwoods, *1616*

Colonial Virginians cooked and enjoyed all sorts of lettuces, cabbages, and leafy greens. The temperate climate and rich soil usually allowed for a long growing season and often produced several harvests a year. Cooking lettuces in soups or stews was a popular way to use an abundant crop, as was cooking them briefly in a hot skillet.

Braised Romaine with Brown Butter and Fennel Seeds

Serves 6

3 romaine lettuce hearts, rinsed and
    trimmed of any bruised outer leaves
2 tablespoons extra-virgin olive oil
2 tablespoons butter
1 tablespoon fennel seeds
1/2 teaspoon salt
1/4 teaspoon freshly ground black
    pepper
juice of 1 lemon (about 2 tablespoons)

Cut the romaine lengthwise through the middle.

Heat the olive oil in a large skillet over medium-high heat. Add the butter and, while stirring, allow it to brown.

Sprinkle in the fennel seeds and stir constantly, allowing the fennel seeds to fry briefly in the brown butter.

Add the romaine cut side up and season with the salt and black pepper. Allow the romaine to brown and turn it in the butter mixture so the fennel seeds mix throughout the leaves. Reduce the heat to medium and cook for about 6 minutes, or until the romaine is fully cooked without falling apart.

Drizzle the romaine with the lemon juice.

Place the romaine on a platter, and pour the remaining juices on top.

The rutabaga, often referred to as a yellow turnip or Swedish turnip, is believed to have originated during the Middle Ages as a cross between white turnips and cabbages and thrives in northern climates. The Old Norse derivation for rutabaga, "rot baggi," meant root bag. And before refrigeration, icehouses, springhouses, and root cellars kept bags of root vegetables fresh. Easy to prepare and highly nutritious, this vegetable dish is thickened with potatoes and sweetened with carrots.

Buttermilk Mashed Rutabagas

Serves 6 to 8

3 pounds rutabagas, peeled and cut into 1-inch pieces

1 large carrot, peeled and cut into 3/4-inch disks

1 medium onion, chopped (about 1 cup)

2 small white potatoes, peeled and cut into 1-inch pieces (about 1 1/2 cups)

1/2 cup buttermilk

8 tablespoons (1 stick) butter, cut into eighths

2 cloves garlic, minced (about 2 teaspoons)

1 1/2 teaspoons salt

1/2 teaspoon freshly ground black pepper

Place the rutabagas, carrots, onions, and potatoes in a large saucepan. Pour in enough cold water to cover by 1 inch and bring to a boil over high heat.

Reduce the heat to medium high. Cover the saucepan and cook for 40 to 45 minutes, or until the rutabagas are tender.

Drain and return the vegetables to the saucepan.

Add the buttermilk, butter, garlic, salt, and black pepper to the saucepan over low heat until the butter has melted. Whip the vegetable mixture with an electric mixer for 2 to 3 minutes, or until relatively smooth.

Adjust the seasoning to taste and serve immediately (see page 48).

Discovered in the West Indies by Christopher Columbus, sweet potatoes were brought to the American mainland in the early sixteenth century. By midcentury, American Indians were cultivating "batatas" in their gardens. For a sweet, rich-flavored sweet potato, select the darker variety. This mashed sweet potato recipe captures the essence of good Southern holiday fare. Baked after mashing, this version is a good make-ahead recipe.

"Bourboned" Mashed Sweet Potatoes

Serves 8

4 pounds sweet potatoes, peeled and
    quartered
8 tablespoons (1 stick) butter, melted
1/2 cup light cream, or half-and-half
1 egg, slightly beaten
1/3 to 1/2 cup bourbon
1/2 cup orange juice
4 tablespoons light brown sugar
2 teaspoons cinnamon
1/2 teaspoon nutmeg
1 teaspoon salt

Butter a 2-quart baking dish.

Place the sweet potatoes in a large saucepan. Pour in enough cold water to cover by 1 inch and bring to a boil over high heat. Reduce the heat to medium high. Cook the sweet potatoes for 25 minutes, or until soft.

Preheat the oven to 350 degrees.

Drain the sweet potatoes and place them into a large mixing bowl. Beat the sweet potatoes using an electric mixer on medium-low speed until smooth.

Add the butter, cream, egg, bourbon, orange juice, light brown sugar, cinnamon, nutmeg, and salt, and beat on medium speed until thoroughly mixed.

Put the sweet potatoes in the baking dish and bake for 20 to 25 minutes, or until thoroughly heated (see page 38).

This thickened custard was originally called "dripping pudding," signifying its placement in the hearth under a large joint of meat roasting from a spit. The pudding would sizzle by the fire while being basted by the dripping fat. This recipe, a slightly more healthful version, uses very hot browned butter. The Yorkshire pudding batter, which is the same for popovers, is always better made in advance.

Buttery Yorkshire Pudding

Serves 6

3 eggs
1½ cups milk
1¼ cups all-purpose flour
1 teaspoon salt
1 tablespoon sugar
½ teaspoon freshly ground black
    pepper
¼ teasopoon grated nutmeg
4 tablespoons (½ stick) butter, divided

Beat the eggs with the milk in a large bowl.

Whisk in the flour, salt, sugar, black pepper, and nutmeg, creating a batter.

Melt and stir in 1 tablespoon of the butter.

Refrigerate the batter for 2 hours, or allow it to stand at room temperature for at least 30 minutes.

Preheat the oven to 450 degrees and place a 1½- to 2-quart baking dish in the oven. Allow the baking dish to heat in the oven for 5 minutes after the oven is preheated.

Add the remaining butter to the baking dish. It should sizzle and begin to brown. Once the butter has completely browned, briefly stir the batter and pour it into the baking dish.

Cook for 15 minutes, turn down the heat to 375 degrees, and cook another 10 minutes, or until the pudding has risen on the sides and is firm in the middle. Serve immediately (see page 44).

A Yorkshire Pudding . . . is an exceeding good Pudding, the Gravy of the Meat eats well with it.
        —Hannah Glasse, The Art of Cookery, 1747

Ever since slaves brought these little legumes with them from Africa, black-eyed peas have been a popular Southern staple. Traditionally, a dish of stewed black-eyed peas eaten on New Year's Day brought luck and prosperity for the coming year. A spoonful of the grilled red onions adds just the right kick to this recipe. Make the pickled onions a day ahead.

Black-Eyed Peas with Grilled Red Onion Pickle

Serves 8

For the red onion pickle
2 medium red onions, peeled and sliced into round, 1/4-inch-thick slabs
1/2 cup red wine vinegar
1 teaspoon salt
1/2 teaspoon hot red pepper flakes
1/2 teaspoon mustard seed
1/4 teaspoon celery seed
1/2 teaspoon turmeric
2 tablespoons sugar

For the black-eyed peas
1 store-bought smoked ham hock
1 medium onion, finely chopped (about 1 cup)
1 tablespoon chopped garlic
1 tablespoon molasses
1 (14-ounce) can diced tomatoes with their juices
1 1/2 teaspoons salt
1/2 teaspoon freshly ground black pepper
1 pound black-eyed peas, rinsed, soaked overnight, and drained
sour cream (optional), for garnish

Grill the onion slabs on both sides on a charcoal or gas grill over medium-high heat for 3 to 4 minutes on each side, or until caramelized. Place them into a small saucepan.

Add the red wine vinegar, salt, hot red pepper flakes, mustard seed, celery seed, turmeric, and sugar, and cover the saucepan. Bring to a boil and reduce the heat to medium. Cook uncovered for 30 minutes, or until the onions are tender.

Remove from the stove and allow to cool. Transfer the red onion pickle to a clean jar and refrigerate.

Place the ham hock in a large saucepan and cover with 6 cups water. Cook the ham hock over medium-high heat for 30 minutes.

Add the onions, garlic, molasses, diced tomatoes with their juices, salt, black pepper, and black-eyed peas.

Bring to a boil and reduce the heat to medium low. Cover and simmer for 1 1/2 to 2 hours, or until tender, stirring occasionally.

Dish up the black-eye peas with the red onion pickle or offer the pickle as a side dish and garnish with sour cream, if desired (see page 52).

Breads and Stuffings

Always keep by you two or more Pounds of the
Dough of your last baking, well cover'd with Flour
to make Leaven to serve from one baking Day to
another; the more Leaven is put to the Flour the
lighter and spongier the Bread will be, the fresher
the Leaven, the Bread will be less sour.

—Hannah Glasse, *The Art of Cookery*, 1747

Recipes for stollen, the traditional German bread known as "Christstollen," date back to the 1500s. The classic folded-over shape of the dough is symbolic of the swaddling of baby Jesus. Always rich with butter, slightly sweet with dried and candied fruit, and well preserved with brandy or rum, stollen is a treasured gift for the holiday table.

Williamsburg Christmas Stollen

Serves 8 to 10

1/3 cup golden raisins

1/3 cup dried sweetened cranberries

1/3 cup candied citron, or fruitcake candies with no red or green

1 teaspoon grated lemon peel

3/4 cup golden rum

1 tablespoon rum flavoring

1 package active dry yeast (2 1/4 teaspoons)

1/2 cup warm milk

2 tablespoons sugar

8 tablespoons (1 stick) butter, melted (not hot)

1 egg plus 1 yolk, beaten

2 1/2 cups plus 2 tablespoons all-purpose flour, sifted and divided

1 teaspoon salt

1 teaspoon allspice

1 teaspoon cinnamon

1/2 cup sliced almonds, toasted (about 3 ounces)

1/2 to 3/4 cup confectioners' sugar, for dusting

Soak the raisins, cranberries, candied citron, and lemon peel in the rum and rum flavoring and let stand for at least 1 hour.

Dissolve the yeast in the warm milk and sugar in a medium bowl and let stand 10 minutes.

Add the butter and eggs and mix.

Combine 2 1/2 cups flour, and the salt, allspice, cinnamon, and almonds in a large bowl.

Make a well in the flour mixture. Add the yeast mixture into the center of the well and slowly mix together, forming a smooth dough.

Knead the dough for 2 minutes by hand. Form the dough into a ball, cover, and allow it to rise about 1 hour, or until doubled in size.

Strain the fruit mixture, reserving the rum.

Dust the fruit mixture with the remaining flour and knead the fruit mixture into the dough.

Shape the dough into an oval, about 1/2-inch thick by 12 inches long and 6 inches wide. Fold the top edge down to within 1/2 inch of the bottom edge, resembling a turnover or folded omelet, and gently seal the seam using a little water, creating the classic stollen shape.

Gently push down on the loaf so it is of uniform thickness. Transfer to a buttered heavy-duty baking sheet, cover, and allow to rise 45 minutes.

Preheat the oven to 375 degrees. Bake the loaf for 25 to 30 minutes, or until it is lightly browned and sounds hollow when tapped. Transfer the bread to cool on a wire rack.

Brush all sides of the stollen with the reserved rum, allowing it to soak in, and dust generously with the confectioners' sugar.

Store the stollen in an airtight container with plenty of additional confectioners' sugar.

Scones are an early Scottish quick bread, in many ways resembling a sweeter version of a good Southern biscuit. Like biscuits, make these by hand in a bowl with a wooden spoon the old-fashioned way. Serve with clotted cream or sour cream and good preserves.

Cranberry and Pecan Scones

Makes 8 to 12

2 cups all-purpose flour
1 tablespoon baking powder
1/2 teaspoon baking soda
1 teaspoon salt
1/4 cup packed light brown sugar
8 tablespoons (1 stick) very cold butter
1/2 cup dried sweetened cranberries
1/2 cup chopped pecans (about
    3 ounces)
1 egg, beaten
1/3 cup light cream, or half-and-half
milk, for brushing
granulated sugar, for sprinkling

Preheat the oven to 425 degrees.

Sift the flour, baking powder, and baking soda into a large bowl. Mix in the salt and light brown sugar.

Grate the butter onto the flour mixture using a cheese grater. Break the butter into smaller pieces evenly throughout the flour mixture using your hands, until the flour mixture resembles coarse meal.

Add the cranberries and pecans and mix just until combined. Make a well into the center of the flour mixture.

Add the egg and cream to the well and mix quickly. Add a little more cream if necessary to bring the dough away from the side of the bowl.

Turn the dough out onto a floured surface and knead three to four times. Form the dough into two equal-size balls. Roll out each ball on the floured surface into a circle 1/2-inch thick. Cut the dough into wedges and place on a nonstick baking sheet 1/2-inch apart. Brush the tops of the wedges with milk and sprinkle on the granulated sugar. Bake for 12 to 15 minutes. This recipe is pictured with Gingered Pumpkin Muffins (see page 88).

Batter breads, or quick breads, were almost always cooked flat on a griddle like a pancake. Late in the eighteenth century, however, griddle cakes started to change their shape and texture. With the American discovery of the leavening properties of potash, also known as pearl ash (a crude form of potassium carbonate), people began adding it to bread recipes. The newfound ability to raise breads without yeast led to all kinds of new shapes in bakeware, forever blessing the world with muffin pans. Amelia Simmons's 1796 American Cookery, *the first cookbook written by an American, features "pearlash" in several recipes including her "Gingerbread." This preparation uses baking powder, the modern refinement of carbonate from wood ash.*

Gingered Pumpkin Muffins

Makes 16

3 cups all-purpose flour
1 tablespoon baking powder
1/2 teaspoon baking soda
1 tablespoon cinnamon
1 teaspoon ground ginger
1 teaspoon salt
12 tablespoons (1 1/2 sticks) butter
1 cup granulated sugar
3 eggs
1 (15-ounce) can pumpkin (2 cups)
1 1/2 cups milk
1 tablespoon oatmeal
1 tablespoon chopped walnuts
   (optional)
1 tablespoon light brown sugar

Preheat the oven to 450 degrees. Butter and dust the muffin pan with flour.

Sift the flour, baking powder, baking soda, cinnamon, ginger, and salt into a large bowl.

Beat the butter with the granulated sugar in a large mixing bowl with an electric mixer on medium-high speed for 2 to 3 minutes, or until creamy.

Add the eggs one at a time with the electric mixer on low speed. Increase the speed to high and whip 1 to 2 minutes, or until smooth.

Add the pumpkin and milk and blend on low speed for 1 minute, or until smooth.

Make a well in the middle of the flour mixture. Add the pumpkin mixture and mix together just until the flour mixture is thoroughly blended. Do not over mix.

Spoon the muffin mixture into the muffin pan, filling the cups to the top.

Mix the oatmeal, walnuts, if desired, and light brown sugar together in a small bowl. Sprinkle 1/2 teaspoon of the oatmeal mixture on each muffin.

Bake for 10 minutes, then reduce the heat to 375 degrees and bake for an additional 12 to 15 minutes, or until an inserted toothpick comes out clean (see page 86).

The very first U.S. patent ever granted was for an improved method "in the making of Pot ash." The patent was signed by President George Washington and Secretary of State Thomas Jefferson. Mary Randolph's early American cookbook includes a recipe for soda cake that is reminiscent of today's popular Southern-style biscuit. "Dissolve half a pound of sugar in a pint of milk; add a teaspoonful of soda, pour it on two pounds of flour— melt half a pound of butter, knead all together till light." These biscuits are good with the main holiday meal or for breakfast, but always delicious slathered with butter.

Applesauce Buttermilk Biscuits

Makes 12

2¹/₂ cups all-purpose flour
1 tablespoon baking powder
¹/₄ teaspoon baking soda
1 tablespoon sugar
1¹/₂ teaspoons salt
1 teaspoon cinnamon
¹/₂ teaspoon allspice
6 tablespoons (³/₄ stick) very cold
    butter
1 egg, slightly beaten
¹/₂ cup applesauce
¹/₂ cup plus 2 tablespoons buttermilk,
    divided
cinnamon, for sprinkling

Preheat the oven to 450 degrees.

Sift the flour, baking powder, baking soda, sugar, salt, cinnamon, and allspice into a large bowl.

Grate the butter onto the flour mixture using a cheese grater. Break the butter into smaller pieces evenly throughout the flour mixture using your hands, until the flour mixture resembles coarse meal.

Make a well in the flour mixture. Add the egg, applesauce, and ¹/₂ cup of the buttermilk into the center of the well and mix just until the dough holds together.

Turn the dough out onto a floured surface and briefly knead. Roll or hand form the dough into a rectangle ¹/₂-inch thick by 8 inches long and 6 inches wide, using some additional flour, if necessary.

Cut the dough into 2-inch rectangles and place them on an ungreased baking sheet ¹/₂-inch apart. Decoratively pierce the top of each rectangle with the tip of a fork.

Brush the tops of the rectangles with the remaining buttermilk and sprinkle with cinnamon.

Bake for 12 to 14 minutes, or until golden brown (see page 60).

Acorns were good till Bread was found.
—Francis Bacon, Of the Colours of
Good and Evil, 1691

At Southern tables, holiday meals are incomplete without corn bread. Tradition dictates that a butter-slathered wedge of corn bread accompany cooked greens, black-eyed peas, or stewed cabbage. Settlers learned from American Indians to cook corn "ashcakes" directly on fireside rocks, and adapted the concept to cornmeal mush cooked on iron hoes, creating hoecakes. In eighteenth-century Williamsburg, cooking corn-based batter breads in a well-seasoned cast-iron skillet by the hearth was popular. Cast iron conducts heat evenly and provides the necessary golden, crispy crust so essential for tasty corn bread. This wonderful, all-purpose recipe is good for corn sticks, griddle cakes, or stuffing.

Skillet-Baked Corn Bread

Serves 4 to 6

1¾ cups stone-ground yellow
   cornmeal
1 tablespoon sugar
1 teaspoon salt
1 teaspoon baking powder
1 teaspoon baking soda
1 egg
2 cups buttermilk
1 tablespoon butter

Place a well-seasoned 10-inch cast-iron skillet in the oven. Preheat the oven to 450 degrees.

Place the cornmeal, sugar, and salt in a medium bowl. Sift in the baking powder and baking soda and mix together.

Add the egg and buttermilk into the cornmeal mixture just until mixed.

Five minutes after the oven reaches 450 degrees, remove the skillet from the oven, immediately add the butter, and stir carefully.

Once the melted butter is sizzling and begins to brown, add the cornmeal batter into the hot skillet. Bake for 10 to 12 minutes, or until a toothpick inserted into the center comes out clean.

Carefully turn the corn bread out onto a large, round platter or cutting board, presenting the corn bread bottom-side up. Serve fresh and warm with butter, syrup, or honey.

[There] are old Indian fields of exceedingly rich Land, that beare two Crops of Indian Corne a yeare.
  —*Edward Bland,* The Discovery of
  New Brittaine, *1651*

This hearty yeast dough recipe is unlike most quick bread varieties of sweet potato or pumpkin bread. Rich and dark from molasses, this bread is best toasted and buttered or sliced fresh with any holiday meal. So good, it may find its place at the table year-round.

Sweet Potato Raisin Bread

Serves 8 to 10

1 package active dry yeast (2¼ teaspoons)

¼ cup warm milk

3 tablespoons sorghum molasses, or cane

¼ cup vegetable oil

1 cup cooked, peeled, and mashed sweet potatoes

¾ cup raisins

2 teaspoons salt

¾ cup plus 2 tablespoons whole wheat flour

1¾ cups all-purpose flour

1 teaspoon cornmeal, for sprinkling

Lightly oil a 9 by 5 by 3-inch loaf pan.

Dissolve the yeast in the warm milk in a small bowl and let stand 10 minutes. Stir in the molasses and let stand for 5 minutes.

Either transfer the yeast mixture to a large bowl, if mixing by hand, or transfer to the bowl of an electric mixer with the dough hook attachment.

Add the vegetable oil, sweet potatoes, raisins, and salt and mix well. Add the whole wheat flour and all-purpose flour and mix until incorporated.

Either turn the dough out onto a floured surface to knead for 10 minutes by hand and place back into the large bowl, or knead slowly in the electric mixer for 5 minutes.

Cover the dough with a damp towel and allow it to rise in a warm place about 1 hour, or until doubled in size.

Punch down the dough and knead briefly by hand.

Form the dough into a loaf and place it in the loaf pan. Cover with a damp towel and allow it to rise a second time about 45 minutes, or until nearly doubled in size. Preheat the oven to 350 degrees.

Sprinkle the loaf with the cornmeal and bake for 35 to 40 minutes, or until it sounds hollow when tapped.

Allow the bread to rest in the loaf pan 5 minutes. Turn out the bread to cool on a wire rack (see page 48).

Corn bread is truly the original American bread. Since the time American Indians taught early settlers to plant a kernel of corn along with a small fish, providing a healthier crop, corn production has flourished in the rich soil of the New World. Today more land is used to farm corn than any other grain. In many homes it is unthinkable to use any other bread for the dressing or stuffing that accompanies a holiday feast. The addition of mushrooms and chestnuts contribute rich, earthy flavors with a touch of nutty sweetness. If chestnuts are not available, substitute any other favorite nut-meat.

Corn Bread, Mushroom, and Chestnut Stuffing

Serves 8

1 Skillet-Baked Corn Bread recipe
  (see page 90)
3 tablespoons butter
1 medium onion, finely chopped
  (about 1 cup)
1 cup finely chopped celery
4 ounces button mushrooms, or
  crimini, rinsed and chopped (about
  1 cup)
1 teaspoon fresh thyme, or 1/2 teaspoon
  dried
1/2 teaspoon rubbed dried sage
1 cup chestnuts, roasted, peeled, and
  chopped (about 8 ounces)
2 tablespoons chopped parsley
1/2 teaspoon salt
1/2 teaspoon freshly ground black
  pepper
1 egg, beaten
1 1/2 cups turkey broth, or low-sodium
  chicken broth, or vegetable broth

Prepare the corn bread.

Preheat the oven to 350 degrees and butter a 2-quart baking dish.

Melt the butter in a large skillet over medium-high heat. Add the onions and celery and cook, stirring often, for 4 to 5 minutes, or until soft.

Reduce the heat to medium and add the mushrooms, thyme, and sage and cook until the mushrooms are tender. Add the chestnuts, parsley, salt, and black pepper and cook for 1 minute and remove from the heat.

Separately crumble the corn bread in a large bowl.

Pour the cooked vegetable mixture onto the corn bread and mix. Stir in the egg, moisten the stuffing with the broth, and mix well.

Transfer the stuffing to the baking dish and cook for 30 to 35 minutes, or until lightly browned (see page 51).

From time immemorial oysters have been harvested from the Chesapeake Bay and its estuaries. Because of their abundance, it is no wonder these delectable bivalves made their way into many recipes, including soups, stews, and baked puddings. This quick and easy preparation is wonderful as a side dish or the featured dressing.

Oyster and Cracker Crumb Dressing

Serves 4

5 tablespoons butter, divided
1/2 cup chopped green bell pepper
1/2 cup chopped celery
1 clove garlic, minced (about
   1 teaspoon)
1/2 cup chopped green onions
2 cups crushed saltine crackers
1/4 teaspoon cayenne pepper
1 teaspoon lemon juice
2 teaspoons Worcestershire sauce
1 pint oysters with their liquor

Preheat the oven to 350 degrees and butter a 1-quart baking dish.

Melt 4 tablespoons of the butter in a medium saucepan over medium-high heat.

Add the green bell peppers and celery and cook for 4 to 5 minutes, or until soft.

Stir in the garlic and green onions and cook for 1 minute. Remove the saucepan from the stove.

Mix the saltine crackers with the celery mixture in a medium bowl.

Add the cayenne pepper, lemon juice, and Worcestershire sauce, and mix.

Add the oysters with their liquor and gently mix together. Place the oyster mixture in the baking dish and dot with the remaining butter.

Bake for 25 to 30 minutes, or until the oysters are heated through and firm.

This dressing is an excellent accompaniment to Roasted Brined Turkey with Pan-Drip Gravy (see page 38).

Sometimes with oysters we combine,
Sometimes assist the sav'ry chine.
From the low peasant to the lord,
The turkey smoaks on ev'ry board.
           —*John Gay, "The Turkey and the Ant," Fables, 1727*

Before history was recorded, American Indians were harvesting wild rice in the northern regions of this vast continent and pine nuts from the cones of the piñon tree in the West. Celebrating the bountiful harvest, this recipe harmonizes the nutty flavors of wild rice and pine nuts beautifully. The date palm is one of the oldest fruit trees in the world, historically called the "tree of life." In this stuffing, dates add a rich, sweet flavor so familiar with holiday fare. This wonderful alternative to traditional bread stuffings becomes a very quick recipe if the wild rice is cooked beforehand.

Wild Rice Stuffing with Toasted Pine Nuts and Dates

Serves 6

1/2 cup wild rice, rinsed
3 tablespoons butter
1/2 cup finely chopped onion
1/2 cup finely chopped celery
1/2 cup pine nuts
1/2 cup chopped unsweetened dates
1 apple, peeled, cored, and grated
   (about 3/4 cup)
1 cup orange juice
1/2 teaspoon dried thyme
1/4 teaspoon dried sage
1 teaspoon salt
1/4 teaspoon freshly ground black
   pepper
2 cups dried bread crumbs

To prepare the wild rice

Place the wild rice and 2 cups water in a heavy, small saucepan over high heat. Bring to a boil. Reduce the heat to low. Partially cover the saucepan and cook the wild rice for 50 to 60 minutes, or until the wild rice has puffed.

Remove the wild rice from the stove and cover the saucepan tightly. Allow the wild rice to rest for 10 minutes.

Drain off excess water and set the wild rice aside.

To prepare the stuffing

Melt the butter in a large skillet over medium-high heat.

Add the onions and celery and cook about 4 to 5 minutes, or until tender.

Increase the heat to high and add the pine nuts, stirring constantly, about 3 to 4 minutes, or until they begin to brown.

Add the cooked wild rice, dates, grated apple, and orange juice. Cook for 3 minutes, or until the wild rice mixture is heated through, stirring occasionally.

Add the thyme, sage, salt, and black pepper and mix. Cook for 2 minutes.

Toss in the bread crumbs and mix together.

Place the stuffing in the cavity of your favorite holiday bird or heat separately in a baking dish (see page 56).

Desserts, Cookies, and Confections

On Thursday the 26th of decem. Mama

made 6 mince pies, & 7 custards, 12 tarts . . .

for the ball.

—Sally Cary Fairfax, Christmas 1771

Certain tropical fruits were easily transported to the American colonies during colder months, including coconuts, which were always a mysterious yet pleasant surprise to the tidewater table. The frosting for this recipe, while not technically a "boiled icing," is cooked over simmering water, creating a fluffy, satiny meringue.

Snowflake Coconut Cake

Serves 10 to 12

To make the cake

3 cups cake flour
1 tablespoon baking powder
$1/2$ teaspoon salt
1 cup buttermilk
8 tablespoons (1 stick) butter
3 eggs
4 egg yolks, reserving the egg whites
  for the frosting recipe
$11/2$ cups sugar
1 teaspoon vanilla extract
$1/2$ cup almonds, toasted and chopped
  (about 2 ounces)
2 cups flaked coconut

Preheat the oven to 350 degrees. Butter three 8-inch round baking pans and dust with flour.

Sift the flour, baking powder, and salt together.

Heat the buttermilk and butter in a small saucepan over medium heat until the butter has melted. Keep warm.

Place the eggs, egg yolks, and sugar in a mixing bowl and beat with an electric mixer on medium-high speed for 4 to 5 minutes, or until fluffy.

Alternately add some of the flour mixture and some of the buttermilk mixture to the egg mixture with the mixer on low speed until incorporated. Beat on medium speed until well mixed. Mix in the vanilla extract and almonds.

Pour the cake batter into the pans evenly. The pans will be only about one-third full. Bake for 18 to 20 minutes, or until an inserted toothpick comes out clean.

Cool the cakes in the pans for 10 minutes before turning them out onto wire racks. Meanwhile, prepare the frosting.

Layer and cover the cake with the frosting. Sprinkle and lightly push the coconut onto the sides and top of the cake. Allow the cake to set after it is frosted for at least 2 hours before serving.

For the frosting

4 reserved egg whites (from the cake
  recipe)
$11/2$ cups sugar
4 tablespoons cold water
$1/2$ teaspoon cream of tartar
$1/2$ teaspoon almond extract

Combine the egg whites, sugar, water, and cream of tartar in a heatproof medium bowl.

Place the bowl over a saucepan of barely simmering water. Beat with an electric mixer on low speed 3 to 4 minutes, or until fluffy. Beat on medium-high speed for 6 to 7 minutes, or until very thick meringue forms.

Remove from the heat, add the almond extract, and beat on high about 3 minutes, or until peaks hold their shape.

The eighteenth-century American chestnut tree produced a sweet and meaty nut loaded with protein. The original species is all but extinct throughout the eastern United States; however, other varieties are readily available during the holiday season.

Chocolate Fudge Chestnut Torte with Gingersnap Crust

Serves 8

To prepare the gingersnap crust
1 (16-ounce) package gingersnaps, ground (about 3 cups)
2 tablespoons sugar
8 tablespoons (1 stick) butter, melted

For the torte
12 ounces bittersweet chocolate, or semisweet (about 2 cups chocolate chips), divided
3/4 cup sugar, divided
6 egg yolks, reserving the egg whites
1 1/2 cups chestnut puree
1/2 cup all-purpose flour
1/8 teaspoon salt
1/2 cup heavy cream
whipped cream (optional), for decoration

Combine the gingersnaps, sugar, and butter in a medium bowl. Press the gingersnap mixture into the bottom and halfway up the sides of a 10-inch springform pan.

————————

Preheat the oven to 350 degrees.

Melt half the chocolate in a small bowl over barely simmering water.

Beat 1/2 cup of the sugar and the egg yolks in a medium mixing bowl with an electric mixer on high speed for about 4 minutes, or until light and fluffy. Add the chestnut puree and mix on medium speed for 2 to 3 minutes, or until smooth. Add the melted chocolate, flour, and salt, and mix briefly until smooth.

Separately, beat the remaining sugar and the reserved egg whites in a mixing bowl with an electric mixer (with clean beaters) on high speed for 4 to 5 minutes, or until a meringue with soft peaks forms.

Mix one-fourth of the meringue into the chestnut mixture to lighten it. Gently and briefly fold in the remaining meringue.

Immediately pour the torte batter into the springform pan. Place the pan on a baking sheet to catch any melting butter from the crust.

Bake for 50 to 55 minutes, or until an inserted toothpick comes out clean. Cool the torte in the pan on a wire rack for at least 1 hour.

Place the remaining chocolate into a heatproof medium bowl.

Carefully bring the heavy cream to a boil over medium-high heat and immediately pour over the chocolate. Stir the chocolate mixture with a whisk until the chocolate has melted to a pourable consistency.

Pour the chocolate mixture on top of the torte and spread evenly. Allow the torte to cool to room temperature.

For a finishing touch, blend any extra chestnut puree with whipped cream. Decorate each slice of the torte, or serve on the side (see page 98).

There are many mentions of triflelike recipes throughout the centuries. Soaking dried cake and breads in various liquors and then layering them with custard cream and prepared fruit became a popular dessert. Though some slow-ripening fruit was brought up from the Caribbean during colonial winters, most settlers would have used varieties that had been "put up." This recipe uses fresh and prepared fruit, including kiwifruit and pineapple. Be sure to display the dessert in a glass trifle bowl or individual glasses so everyone may appreciate the colorful fruit and custard cream layers.

Christmas Trifle

Serves 16

For the custard cream
2¹/₂ cups milk
¹/₃ cup granulated sugar
3 tablespoons cornstarch
5 egg yolks
1 tablespoon vanilla extract
2 cups heavy cream
¹/₄ cup confectioners' sugar

Heat the milk in a small saucepan over medium-high heat until barely simmering.

Separately, mix the granulated sugar, cornstarch, and egg yolks with a pinch of salt in a heavy-bottomed medium saucepan over medium heat.

Whisk in the hot milk slowly, about ¹/₂ cup at a time, until all the milk is incorporated into the egg mixture. Stir constantly with a wooden spoon and cook for 12 to 15 minutes, or until lumps of custard begin to form. Lower the heat and whisk until smooth.

Remove from the heat and mix in the vanilla extract.

Transfer the custard to a large bowl. Cover the bowl with plastic, poke a few holes in the plastic, and cool.

Place the heavy cream and confectioners' sugar in a medium mixing bowl. Whip on medium speed for 4 to 5 minutes, or until stiff peaks form, and refrigerate. Reserve 2 tablespoons of the whipped cream for decoration.

Once the custard has cooled, mix in one-third of the whipped cream with the custard using a rubber spatula to lighten. Gently fold in the remaining whipped cream and refrigerate the custard cream.

For the trifle

1¹/₂ pounds vanilla or lemon pound
    cake, sliced ¹/₂-inch thick

1 cup raspberry jam

4 ounces dry sherry

10 kiwifruit, peeled and cut into
    ¹/₈-inch slices, reserving several
    slices for decoration

1 (24-ounce) container pineapple, or
    mango, drained and cut in chunks
    (in the fresh fruit section)

2 (10-ounce) containers frozen straw-
    berries with their juices, thawed,
    reserving 1 berry for decoration

¹/₄ cup sliced almonds, toasted (about
    1 ounce), for decoration

Preheat the oven to 350 degrees.

Lay the pound cake on baking sheets and bake about 10 minutes, or until partially dried. Remove from the oven and cool. Spread each slice of pound cake with a thin layer of raspberry jam.

Place a layer of pound cake slices, breaking them to fit evenly, into an 8-inch-deep trifle bowl, or 3-quart glass bowl. Drizzle one-third of the sherry onto the pound cake.

Line the edge of the bowl with the kiwifruit, leaving a slight gap between each slice. Fill in the gaps with chunks of pineapple. Spoon on one-third of the strawberries with their juices, making some visible through the kiwifruit.

Add additional kiwifruit, pineapple, and strawberries to level out the layer.

Add in and spread evenly one-third of the custard cream.

Repeat this layering process twice, ending with a layer of custard cream on top.

Decorate with the reserved whipped cream, kiwifruit, strawberry, and the toasted almonds.

For individual portions, layer the glasses proportionately and decorate each serving (see page 101).

At Christmas play, and make good chear,
For Christmas comes but once a year.
    —Thomas Tusser, "The Farmers daily diet,"
    Five Hundred Points of Good Husbandry, *1577*

Call them cobblers, buckles, pandowdies, crisps, grunts, or slumps—they are all old recipes that combine baked fruit with some kind of topping or breadlike filling. North American blueberries baked with firm, tart apples and a crisp crumble topping makes this comforting recipe an American favorite.

Apple and Blueberry Crumble

Serves 8

For the filling
8 Granny Smith apples, peeled, cored, and cut in eighths
1 teaspoon chopped lemon zest
juice of 1 lemon (about 3 tablespoons)
$1/2$ cup all-purpose flour
2 tablespoons cornstarch
$1/4$ cup granulated sugar
$1/4$ cup packed light brown sugar
1 teaspoon cinnamon
$1/4$ teaspoon allspice
$1/4$ teaspoon nutmeg
$1/8$ teaspoon salt
2 cups fresh whole blueberries, or frozen
mint leaf, for garnish

Preheat the oven to 400 degrees. Lightly butter a 2-quart baking dish.

Place the apples in a large bowl and toss with the lemon zest and lemon juice.

Place the flour, cornstarch, granulated sugar, light brown sugar, cinnamon, allspice, nutmeg, and salt in a food processor with the blade attachment. Mix together.

Toss the apples in the flour mixture and place the apples into the baking dish, pressing them down snugly.

Top with the blueberries. Do not mix the fruit.

Meanwhile, prepare the crumble topping.

Sprinkle the crumble topping over the blueberries. Bake for 50 to 55 minutes, or until golden brown and the apples are soft.

Garnish with a mint leaf and serve with cool cream or ice cream.

For the crumble topping
$1/4$ cup packed light brown sugar
$1/4$ cup granulated sugar
1 teaspoon cinnamon
$1/4$ teaspoon allspice
$1/4$ teaspoon nutmeg
$1/8$ teaspoon salt
$3/4$ cup all-purpose flour
8 tablespoons (1 stick) cold butter, cut into small pieces

Place the light brown sugar, granulated sugar, cinnamon, allspice, nutmeg, salt, and flour in a food processor with the blade attachment. Mix well.

Add the cold butter. Pulse in the butter just until the topping resembles coarse meal. Do not over mix.

Discovered by Columbus on his maiden voyage to the New World in 1492, pumpkins and squash are indigenous to this continent. American Indians enjoyed them cut into strips and grilled by the fire. It did not take long for English colonists to adapt Old World recipes to accommodate this nutritious winter squash, as noted in a 1630 Pilgrim ballad:

> *For pottage and puddings and custards and pies,*
> *Our pumpkins and parsnip are common supplies;*
> *We have pumpkin at morning and pumpkin at noon,*
> *If 'twere not for pumpkins, we should be undone.*

Buttery Rum Pumpkin Pie

Serves 8

1 pie dough recipe (see page 17), or
   1 (9-inch) deep-dish-style piecrust
2 eggs
1/4 cup granulated sugar
1/2 cup packed light brown sugar
2 tablespoons all-purpose flour
1 teaspoon cinnamon
1/2 teaspoon ground ginger
1/4 teaspoon nutmeg
1/2 teaspoon salt
1 teaspoon rum flavoring
1 (15-ounce) can pumpkin (2 cups)
1 teaspoon vanilla extract
2 tablespoons butter, melted
1 cup heavy cream, or evaporated milk
whipped cream, for decoration

Preheat the oven to 450 degrees.

If using homemade pie dough, roll out the dough onto a floured surface large enough to line a deep-dish-style 9-inch pie pan and decoratively crimp the edges. Refrigerate until the oven is fully preheated.

Place the eggs, granulated sugar, and light brown sugar in a large mixing bowl. Beat with an electric mixer on high speed for 2 to 3 minutes, or until frothy. Mix in the flour, cinnamon, ginger, nutmeg, salt, and rum flavoring. Mix in the pumpkin, vanilla extract, and butter.

Add the heavy cream and mix on medium speed for 1 minute.

Pour the pie batter into the dough-lined pan, or piecrust. Immediately turn the oven down to 375 degrees and bake for 60 to 65 minutes, or until the pie is nicely browned and an inserted toothpick comes out clean.

Serve with whipped cream.

The indigenous pecan tree gets it name from the Algonquin word "pacane," which means nuts that must be cracked with a stone. Pecans were quite popular in the colonial capital, and old-growth trees still survive throughout Colonial Williamsburg's Historic Area. Shortbread dates to sixteenth-century Scotland where rich, buttery cookies traditionally brought in the New Year. This classic Southern pecan pie is made creamy with buttermilk and baked atop a flaky, cookielike shortbread crust.

Buttermilk Pecan Pie with Shortbread Crust

Serves 8

For the shortbread dough
12 tablespoons (1¹/₂ sticks) butter,
   room temperature
2 cups all-purpose flour
¹/₂ cup confectioners' sugar
¹/₂ teaspoon salt
1 egg yolk, slightly beaten
1 teaspoon vanilla extract
2 tablespoons cold water

For the pie
8 tablespoons (1 stick) butter, softened
1 cup granulated sugar
³/₄ cup packed light brown sugar
4 eggs
3 tablespoons all-purpose flour
¹/₈ teaspoon salt
1¹/₂ tablespoons lemon juice
2 teaspoons vanilla extract
1 cup buttermilk
2 cups roughly chopped pecans (about
   8 ounces)

Place the butter, flour, sugar, and salt in a medium mixing bowl. Mix together with an electric mixer on medium-high speed for 1 minute, or until it resembles coarse meal.

Add the egg yolk and vanilla extract, and mix on low speed for 1 to 2 minutes, or until well blended.

Sprinkle in the water and form the dough into a ball using your hands. Wrap the dough in plastic, flatten, and refrigerate for 1 hour.

Roll out the shortbread dough onto a floured surface or between two pieces of waxed paper. Place the shortbread dough into a 9-inch pie pan.

Preheat the oven to 350 degrees.

Place the butter, granulated sugar, and light brown sugar in a large mixing bowl. Beat together for 3 to 4 minutes, or until creamy.

Add the eggs one at a time on low speed. Blend in the flour, salt, lemon juice, and vanilla extract on low speed for 1 minute, or just until incorporated. Mix in the buttermilk and pecans until smooth.

Pour the pie mixture into the shortbread-lined pie pan. Bake for 55 to 60 minutes, or until it is golden brown and the center of the pie is set. Cover the edges of the crust with aluminum foil if they begin to get too dark.

Allow the pecan pie to cool on a wire rack.

A nutty-flavored crust of ground walnuts and whole wheat flour is not all that makes this pie so appropriately rustic. The age-old method of folding the bottom pastry up and partially over, leaving the center open, allows an escape of moisture that deliciously intensifies the flavors.

Walnut-Crusted Apple-Cranberry Pie

Serves 8

For the pie dough
1/2 cup walnuts, ground extra fine
1/4 cup whole wheat flour
1 cup all-purpose flour
1 teaspoon salt
8 tablespoons (1 stick) cold butter
1/3 cup ice-cold water

For the pie
5 Granny Smith apples, peeled, cored, and cut into 1-inch pieces (about 5 1/2 cups)
1 teaspoon grated orange zest
1 teaspoon grated lemon zest
1 cup fresh whole cranberries, or frozen
1 cup sugar
1 teaspoon cinnamon
1/4 teaspoon salt
3 tablespoons all-purpose flour
1 tablespoon cornstarch
milk, for brushing
1/4 cup apple jelly

Combine the walnuts, whole wheat flour, all-purpose flour, and salt in a medium bowl. Grate the butter into the bowl using a cheese grater. Break the butter into smaller pieces evenly throughout the flour mixture using your hands. Gradually drizzle in the water, tossing with a fork to mix until the dough holds together in a ball. Wrap the dough in plastic, flatten, and refrigerate.

Preheat the oven to 375 degrees.

Toss together the apples with the orange zest, lemon zest, cranberries, sugar, cinnamon, and salt in a large bowl. Sift the flour and cornstarch together onto the apple mixture and briefly mix. Set aside.

Separately, roll out the dough to a 13-inch circle on a floured 12 by 12-inch piece aluminum foil.

Transfer the dough with the aluminum foil to a baking sheet.

Pour the apple-cranberry filling into the pie shell. Gently push the apple-cranberry filling down, compressing it slightly to ensure a 1 1/2-inch border of dough.

Fold over the perimeter, using the aluminum foil as support, to partially cover the edges of the pie with the dough. Brush the dough with milk and sprinkle with some sugar.

Bake for about 55 to 60 minutes, or until the apples are tender. Cover the edges of the crust with aluminum foil if they begin to get too dark. Allow the pie to cool to room temperature. Remove the aluminum foil and transfer the pie to a serving platter.

Melt the apple jelly in a small saucepan over medium heat or briefly in the microwave. Spoon the melted apple jelly onto the apple-cranberry filling and allow to set, about 20 minutes.

Serve with ice cream or whipped cream with a little additional cinnamon sprinkled on top.

Early American pioneers used more sorghum molasses and honey in their baked goods than any other sweetener. Sorghum cane, originally from Africa, thrives throughout the South. Molasses made from the sorghum cane is still available through a few small suppliers or occasionally at a roadside stand. This dough makes a crisp gingersnap, if cut thin, or a softer version, if cut slightly thicker, that is reminiscent of the famous Raleigh Tavern gingerbread cookie found in Colonial Williamsburg's Historic Area today.

White Chocolate Iced Molasses Cookies

Makes 48

For the cookies
8 tablespoons (1 stick) butter, room temperature
1/2 cup sugar
1/4 teaspoon salt
1 egg, slight beaten
1/2 cup sorghum molasses, or any dark molasses
1/2 teaspoon ground ginger
1/2 teaspoon cinnamon
2 cups all-purpose flour
1 teaspoon baking soda

Place the butter, sugar, and salt in a medium mixing bowl. Beat using an electric mixer on medium speed for 3 to 4 minutes, or until light and fluffy. Mix in the egg, molasses, ginger, and cinnamon.

Sift the flour and baking soda together. Gradually add the flour mixture, 1/2 cup at a time, just until incorporated.

Transfer the dough onto a floured surface and briefly knead. Form the dough into two rectangles, cover with plastic, and refrigerate for 20 to 30 minutes.

Hand roll each rectangle on a floured surface, forming two 10-inch-long, 1- to 11/2- inch diameter tubes. Refrigerate the tubes for at least 4 hours, or overnight.

Preheat the oven to 375 degrees.

Cut the dough into 1/4- to 1/2-inch-thick disks on a lightly floured surface with a flour-dusted sharp knife.

Place the disks onto an ungreased baking sheet 1/2 inch apart. Bake for 6 to 10 minutes, or until browned and firm to the touch. Thin cookies will be more like gingersnaps, requiring less cooking time.

Allow the cookies to cool on the baking sheet.

For the white chocolate icing
6 ounces white chocolate (about 1 cup white chocolate chips)
2 tablespoons butter
2 tablespoons hot water

Melt the white chocolate and butter in a small bowl over barely simmering water.

Add the hot water and stir until smooth. Keep warm.

Drizzle the icing in creative patterns onto the cookies. These cookies are delicious with homemade ice cream (see page 126).

Recipes from the Old World have influenced the culinary culture of the New World time and time again. These Italian cookies, so popular during the holidays, use peanuts instead of almonds. Still warm and flexible immediately after they come out of the oven, you can make all kinds of festive shapes with these cookies.

Peanut Florentines

Makes 16 to 30

12 tablespoons (1½ sticks) butter
1 cup packed light brown sugar
½ cup light corn syrup
1 cup all-purpose flour
dash salt
1 cup unsalted dry roasted peanuts,
    finely chopped

Melt the butter in a medium saucepan over medium-low heat. Add the light brown sugar and corn syrup and stir.

Increase the heat to medium high and bring the butter mixture to a rapid boil.

Remove from the heat and stir in the flour, salt, and peanuts.

Refrigerate the cookie dough for about 45 minutes.

Preheat the oven to 350 degrees. Lightly butter two heavy-duty baking sheets.

Scoop the cookie dough into balls with a small scoop or melon baller. Portioning the scoops from ½ teaspoon to 1 tablespoon will yield cookies ranging from ½ inch to 3 inches. Smaller scoops will require less cooking time. Place the cookie dough balls onto the baking sheets at least 3 to 4 inches apart.

Bake for 8 to 10 minutes, or until the cookies have puddled out, the centers are bubbling, and the edges have browned.

Allow the florentines to cool for 1 to 2 minutes on the baking sheet before removing to shape, or to cool on waxed or parchment paper (see page 112).

Tipsy squires, cakes, and trifles are well-documented recipes in colonial Virginia. This recipe for scrumptious little coconut chocolates—disguised as coconut truffles—are soaked in rum. Eating more than a few could make you tipsy!

Tipsy Coconut Snowball Truffles

Makes 50

1 pound good bittersweet chocolate, or semisweet
1/2 cup heavy cream
4 tablespoons (1/2 stick) butter, softened
1 cup finely ground plain chocolate cookies
1/3 cup dark rum, or golden
1 cup grated coconut, toasted and coarsely chopped
1/2 cup confectioners' sugar, for decoration

Melt the chocolate in a medium bowl over barely simmering water.

Warm the heavy cream in a small saucepan over medium-high heat and add the heavy cream to the melted chocolate.

Add the butter and mix the chocolate mixture until smooth. Remove the chocolate mixture from the heat.

Mix in the cookie crumbs and rum.

Transfer to a small baking dish and refrigerate for 2 to 3 hours, or until the truffle mixture is firm.

Scoop out the truffle mixture with a large melon baller, occasionally dipped in hot water, and form into balls.

Roll the truffles in the coconut and store the truffles in any remaining coconut. Allow the truffles to set in a cool place for at least 2 hours.

Place the truffles on a serving platter and sift the confectioners' sugar directly onto the truffles and platter just prior to serving. Serve at room temperature (see page 112).

I have endeavoured to set out a dessert of sweetmeats, which the industrious house-keeper may lay up in summer at a small expence, and when added to what little fruit is then in season, will make a pretty appearance after the cloth is drawn, and be entertaining to the company.
—Elizabeth Raffald, The Experienced English Housekeeper, *1769*

Cardamom, called the queen of spices, was for centuries an expensive and highly sought after aromatic spice with supposed stimulating effects. In the seventeenth century, many incorrectly believed that mixing cardamom into coffee would perk up the soothing brew! Cut these cookies into any shape and decorate them either for snacks, teatime, or to hang on the tree.

Cardamom Sugar Cookies

Makes 20 to 30

2 cups all-purpose flour
2 tablespoons ground cardamom
1 teaspoon cinnamon
$1/2$ teaspoon nutmeg
$1/8$ teaspoon salt
1 cup (2 sticks) butter, softened
$1/2$ cup granulated sugar
$1/2$ cup confectioners' sugar
1 egg
1 teaspoon vanilla extract
granulated sugar and/or decorating
     sugars (optional), for decoration

Combine the flour, cardamom, cinnamon, nutmeg, and salt in a medium bowl.

Place the butter, granulated sugar, and confectioners' sugar in a large mixing bowl. Beat with an electric mixer on high speed for 3 to 4 minutes, or until light and fluffy.

Mix in the egg and vanilla extract. Scrape the sides and bottom of the bowl and mix again.

Add the flour mixture, $1/2$ cup at a time, on low speed just until blended. Do not over mix. Divide the dough in half, wrap in plastic, and flatten. Refrigerate for 30 minutes, or until firm enough to handle.

Preheat the oven to 375 degrees. Roll the dough out to $1/4$-inch thick. Cut the dough with a floured cutter and place $1^{1}/2$ inches apart on an ungreased baking sheet.

Sprinkle with granulated or decorating sugars, if desired. Bake for 12 to 15 minutes and cool on a wire rack.

God bless the master of this house,
The mistress also,
And all the little children,
That round the table go.
            —*English traditional carol*

Punches, Shrubs, and Cider

Christmas is come, hang on the pot,

Let spits turn round, and ovens be hot;

Beef, pork, and poultry, now provide,

To feast thy neighbours at this tide;

Then wash all down with good wine and beer,

And so with mirth conclude the YEAR.

—*Virginia Almanack,* 1765

"Ves heill," an Old Norse salutation meaning hail, evolved into a toast: "Wassail!" one would say while lifting a glass; "Drinkhail!" would be the response. Wassail, usually a hot seasonal beverage made with fruit, has traditionally been enjoyed at the start of the Christmas season, through New Year's, and finally on Twelfth Night.

Hot Cranberry Wassail

Serves 12

1 (64-ounce) container sweetened cranberry juice, or cranberry juice cocktail
2½ cups apple cider
3 cinnamon sticks
1 teaspoon allspice
½ teaspoon nutmeg
1 tablespoon aromatic bitters
1 cup golden rum (optional)
2 oranges, cut into wedges, for garnish
whole cloves, for garnish
fresh cranberries, for garnish

Combine the cranberry juice, apple cider, cinnamon sticks, allspice, nutmeg, and aromatic bitters in a large saucepan. Bring to a boil over medium-high heat and reduce to a simmer. Cook for 5 minutes.

To serve, pour the wassail into a heatproof serving bowl or traditional wassail bowl and add the rum, if desired. Garnish with the oranges studded with cloves and fresh cranberries.

*Here we come a-wassailing
Among the leaves so green,
Here we come a-wandering
So fair to be seen.
Love and joy come to you
And to your wassail too,
And God bless you, and send you
A happy New Year.*
   —English traditional carol

In colonial Virginia shrubs were popular fruit juice concoctions spiked with alcohol and vinegar. Shrubs have evolved into nonalcoholic fruit juice beverages served over crushed ice, frozen fruit ice, or sorbet. Make the cranberry ice a day ahead and serve this recipe in a punch bowl or individual glasses.

Cranberry Ice and Pineapple Shrubs

Serves 10 to 12

For the cranberry ice
1 (16-ounce) can whole-berry cranberries
2 cups sweetened cranberry juice, or cranberry juice cocktail

For the shrubs
24 ounces soda water
1 quart pineapple juice, preferably fresh, chilled
2 limes, thinly sliced, for garnish

Place the cranberries and cranberry juice in a blender and puree. Pour into ice cube trays, for individual shrubs, or into a 1-quart container for a punch bowl presentation, and freeze.

For a punch bowl presentation, pour the soda water and pineapple juice over the cranberry ice and garnish with lime slices.

For individual shrubs, pour 2 ounces soda water into each glass and top off with pineapple juice, leaving enough room for 1 to 2 cubes cranberry ice.

Add the cranberry ice to each glass and garnish with lime slices.

Allow the cranberry ice to melt and soften a few minutes prior to serving.

One sip of this
Will bathe the drooping spirits in delight
Beyond the bliss of dreams.
—John Milton, Comus, 1637

Frosted Banana and Raspberry Shrubs

Serves 6

2 bananas, sliced
2 cups ice cubes
juice of 1 lemon (about 3 tablespoons)
½ cup apple juice, or pineapple
1 pint raspberry sorbet
mint sprigs, for garnish
orange slices, for garnish

Place the bananas, ice cubes, lemon juice, and apple juice in a blender. Blend on low speed until the ice cubes are crushed. Blend on high speed until thoroughly smooth.

Pour the banana mixture into chilled shrub or wine glasses.

To serve, place one scoop of raspberry sorbet into each glass and garnish with mint and slices of orange (see page 122).

We wish your health, and good fires;
victuals, drink, and good stomachs;
innocent diversion, and good company;
honest trading, and good success;
loving courtship, and good wives;
and lastly, a merry CHRISTMAS *and a happy* NEW YEAR.
—Virginia Almanack, 1771

For as long as wine and brandy have been made from grapes, hard cider has been made from apples. In colonial America cider was the beverage of choice. Cider was distilled into what was called cider spirits, now known as applejack. Mixing a little applejack with nonalcoholic cider gets close to the cider early Americans enjoyed.

Fireside Mulled Cider with Applejack

Serves 10

2 quarts apple cider, preferably fresh
1 cup orange juice
2 cinnamon sticks
2 tablespoons light brown sugar
1 bay leaf
1/2 teaspoon allspice
1/2 teaspoon ground cardamom
1/2 teaspoon nutmeg
1/2 teaspoon ground ginger
1 lemon, sliced
1 orange, peeled in one continuous
   spiral
1 pint applejack (optional)

Combine the apple cider, orange juice, cinnamon sticks, light brown sugar, bay leaf, allspice, cardamom, nutmeg, ginger, lemon slices, and orange peel in a large nonreactive saucepan. Bring to a boil.

Reduce the heat to medium low and steep uncovered for 30 minutes.

Remove the bay leaf.

To serve, pour one ounce applejack, if desired, into a heatproof glass or mug and top off with the cider. Garnish with a cinnamon stick (see page 13).

While briskly to each patriot lip
Walks eager round th' inspiring flip:
Delicious draught, whose pow'rs inherit
The quintessence of public spirit!
   —John Trumbull, *M'Fingal*, 1782

In colonial America rum was a more readily available ingredient to this holiday punch. George Washington enjoyed a recipe of rye whiskey, rum, and sherry but it was not long until the southern favorite of bourbon became the preferred tradition. Floating an icy island in the punch bowl is a deliciously sensible way of keeping these custardy creams nice and cold. Separately these recipes are wonderful, together they are twice as good. Begin to make this a day in advance. The ice cream will need to freeze and the eggnog is a safe cooked custard version that needs to cool.

Spiked Ice Cream Island Eggnog

Serves 12 to 16

For the ice cream
2 cups half-and-half
3 egg yolks
2/3 cup sugar
1 3/4 cups heavy cream
1/2 teaspoon nutmeg
1 teaspoon vanilla extract
1 tablespoon rum flavoring

Bring the half-and-half to a simmer in a saucepan over medium-high heat.

Whisk together the egg yolks and sugar in a small bowl.

Slowly whisk the hot half-and-half into the egg mixture.

Return to the saucepan and cook over medium-low heat, stirring constantly with a wooden spoon, about 10 minutes (making a custard), or until a thermometer reads 145 to 150 degrees.

Remove the custard from the heat and stir in the heavy cream, nutmeg, vanilla extract, and rum flavoring. Transfer to a container and refrigerate at least 2 hours.

Transfer the custard mixture to an ice cream maker and freeze according to manufacturer's directions.

Chill a bowl in the freezer, transfer the ice cream into it, and freeze.

For the eggnog
8 eggs
2 cups milk
3/4 cup sugar
3 cups heavy cream
2 teaspoons vanilla extract
1 cup rum, bourbon, or brandy
1/2 teaspoon nutmeg, for garnish

Place the eggs, milk, sugar, and a pinch of salt into a medium mixing bowl. Beat with an electric mixer on low speed for 2 minutes, or until blended.

Transfer to a medium saucepan and cook over medium heat, stirring constantly with a wooden spoon, for 4 to 5 minutes. Lower the heat to medium low and cook, stirring constantly, for 8 to 10 minutes, or until a thermometer reads 145 to 150 degrees.

Remove from the heat, stir in the heavy cream, vanilla extract, and rum, and whisk until smooth. Refrigerate overnight, or at least for 3 hours.

To serve, place the ice cream in the bottom of a punch bowl, pour on the eggnog, and as soon as the ice cream floats, sprinkle with the nutmeg.

Spanish culinary culture, evident in early recipes for gazpacho and sangria, was well established in colonial America. Because Spanish wines typically were not imported into the English colonies, the popular clarrey wine, known today as claret from Bordeaux, was more commonly enjoyed in sangaree, or sangria. This festive, fruity wine punch, with an added kick from apricot-flavored brandy, is a very refreshing party drink.

Clarrey Sangaree

Serves 12

2 (750-milliliter) bottles dry red wine
1 cup orange juice
1 cup pineapple juice
1 cup apricot-flavored brandy
3 navel oranges, peeled, cut into slices, and quartered
1 lemon, thinly sliced
2 Granny Smith apples, rinsed, cored, and diced, leaving on the peel
dash grated nutmeg
lemon slices, for garnish

Mix together the red wine, orange juice, pineapple juice, brandy, oranges, lemon slices, apples, and nutmeg. Refrigerate at least 2 hours.

Transfer the clarrey sangaree to a sangria pitcher or spouted pitcher. Add about 2 cups ice cubes.

Serve in chilled red wine glasses and garnish with lemon slices.

What harm in drinking can there be,
Since Punch *and life so well agree?*
    —Thomas Blacklock, "On Punch:
    An Epigram," 1746

I have shared with you the light from my Christmas Eve candle.

I have set it in the window of my soul which faces the house

where you dwell.

—W. A. R. Goodwin, Colonial Williamsburg Restoration
visionary, December 24, 1935

Acknowledgments

I want to thank Mary and Donald J. Gonzales, who brought my sisters and me to Colonial Williamsburg in 1958. My wife, Wanda K. Gonzales, graciously stood by me during the entire project and helped me figure out what it was I was trying to say. To my life-long friend and fellow "CW brat" Bobby Jeffrey: you are the only one to call on for real-world editorial assistance.

Thanks also to Joe Rountree, director of Publications, and John Hornback, inventory buyer for Merchandise Management, for deciding it was the right time to pursue a book on holiday fare. I am grateful to Erin Michaela Bendiner, book editor/writer, who somehow made me and the book appear sensibly consistent, contributing insightful suggestions as well as the book's index. I extend my appreciation to Helen M. Olds, senior graphic/book designer and food photography art director. Thank you Tom Green, photographer nonpareil, for focusing on the food. I am appreciative of Cathy B. Hinton, food stylist and photography consultant extraordinaire, and of Sue Rountree, who helped with props and lent her inherent feel for everything Williamsburg to the photo shoot. Many thanks to Julie A. Watson, Publications secretary, for all her assistance in the office and John B. Ogden, research volunteer. I am indebted to Richard McCluney, Royce R. and Kathryn M. Baker vice president for Productions, Publications, and Learning Ventures, and his dedicated staff for all their faith and support of this project.

I am beholden to Barbara Burnett, my sister who got to proofread everything before the other proofreaders got it, and my cousin Clark Taggart, phase-two proofreader and test-photo stylist. Thanks also to Shelly Turner, photo stylist (and my niece!), for all her professional advice. I greatly appreciate the support of my sister Cheryl, who is always there to help in any way.

Finally, I want to acknowledge all the other family food testers who took a risk at the holiday table.

Index

Page numbers in **bold** indicate photographs.